GREAT GARAGES

Sheds & Outdoor Buildings

Plan HPT280036 page 43

145 Projects you can build

Written by
Connie Brown

HOME PLANNERS, LLC
Wholly owned by Hanley-Wood, LLC
Tucson, Arizona

Published by Home Planners, LLC
Wholly owned by Hanley-Wood, LLC
3275 West Ina Road, Suite 110
Tucson, Arizona 85741

Distribution Center:
29333 Lorie Lane
Wixom, Michigan 48393

President—Jayne Fenton
Vice President, Group Content—Jennifer Pearce
Executive Editor—Linda B. Bellamy
Editorial Director—Arlen Feldwick-Jones
Managing Editor—Vicki Frank
Lead Plans Associate—Morenci Wodraska
Plans Associate—Jennifer Lowry
Graphic Designer—Paul Fitzgerald
Graphic Designer—Teralyn Morriss
Senior Production Manager—Sara Lisa
Production Manager—Brenda McClary

Photo Credits
Front cover: ©Peter Aaron/Esto
All rights reserved.
Design by Jay C. Walter, AIA
Entasis Architects, P.C.
Back cover: Allen Maertz Photography

© 1996, 2001
Second Edition, December 2001

10 9 8 7 6 5 4 3 2

Library of Congress Catalog Card
Number: 2001095058

ISBN softcover: 1-881955-98-2

*On the front cover: Design HPT280036 will
be a fantastic addition to your home! Find
a second floor apartment equipped with
a full kitchen, living room, bedroom and
study. See page 43 for more information.*

CONTENTS

Plan HPT280083 page 84

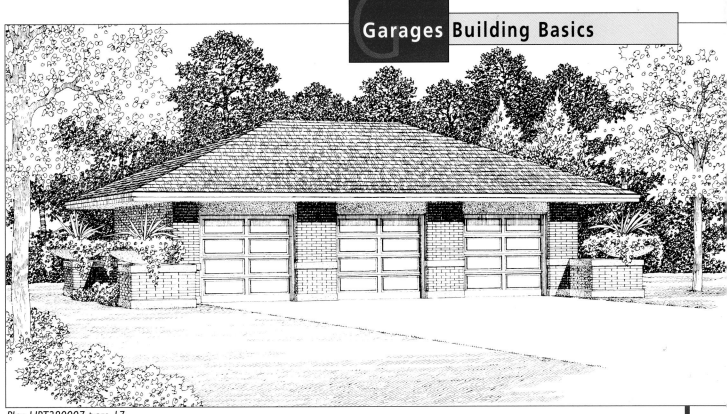

Plan HPT280007 page 17

A garage is the perfect complement to a comfortable home,
serving as a shelter for precious
vehicles, a storage space for tools and
lawn equipment and often as a work
space for the home mechanic. But
sometimes you need more—more
work space, more storage, or even just
more amenities. The projects included
in this book run the gamut from simple,
utilitarian garages to facilities that
accommodate three cars plus office
space or even a complete guest apartment. In addition, there are plans for
sheds, cabanas and pavilions, barns and
stables, and lovely, breezy gazebos. Each
is designed with you in mind and can be
appointed to fit in perfectly with what-
ever style home you have. Best of all,
complete construction blueprints are
available for every plan.

Projects such as those in this book
are very do-able! With an under-
standing of the basics, the right tools for
the job, a set of our plans—plus
an adequate supply of time and
patience—you can create a useful and
practical work area, or a charming and
restful hideaway.

ADVANCE PLANNING

Project Selection

The first step, of course, is to decide
on the project. Of all the possibilities,
what does your home, your property,
your family need the most: a two-car
garage with office space, a whimsical
gazebo, or a practical tool shed?

If you already know what outdoor
structure you want to add to your
property (a garage with a guest suite,
for example) then move right along to
the next easy step. Simply select the
size and layout you prefer from over 20
plans with living space shown in this
book. With all the possibilities fresh in
your mind, take a slow walk around
your property and decide which of the
outdoor structures is the best match in
form and function to your family's
needs and the space and budget you
have available. Then turn to page 153
for order information, and you're on
your way.

You'll also need to consider if you
have the time and expertise to build the
project you've selected, or if you will
need to involve a licensed contractor

for all or part of the work. Once all
that's decided, refer to page 153 to
order the plans you need and turn your
thoughts to site selection.

Site Selection

Site selection depends on a number
of things: what you are building, its
purpose, who is going to use it, its
accessibility, its appeal, and any applicable
building codes and setback.

Location: If you decide to build a
garage, you will want to consider accessibility to the driveway and the house.
You may even decide to connect the
garage to the house via a breezeway. If
your choice is a stable or barn, your
first consideration will be for the animals to be housed there. You'll want
enough room to allow for corrals as
well as some comfortable distance from
the house. If you are building a gazebo,
it will likely become the focal point of
your property and, as such, should
occupy a prominent space.

Drainage: If your property has moist
areas, avoid them if you can. This is par-
ticularly true for gazebos, sheds and
other smaller structures. The alterna-

3

tive is to provide a dry, firm base by adding sand and gravel fill under the project to aid the drainage of the site.

Utilities: Plan ahead for any utilities your project may require: electricity or water for sheds, garages and guesthouses, or gas for heat or a grill. Call your local utilities providers for locations of underground cable and water lines, if necessary.

BUILDING BASICS

Building Permits

When your advance planning and site selection are complete, it's time to obtain the required building permits. Separate building permits are usually needed for each construction discipline: one for the structure, one for the electrical work, one for the plumbing, one for the heating, and so on. Specific requirements for each vary from region to region across the country. Check with your local building officials before you begin your project to determine which permits you need. If your project is small, permits may not be required.

Building Codes

Along with building permits come the codes which must be met. These codes are usually imposed by county or city governments. Codes are required to ensure that your project meets all standards for safety and construction methods. A local inspector will usually check the progress of your project at

> *Check with your local building officials before you begin your project to determine which permits you need.*

various stages, and there could be more than one inspector, depending on the utilities you incorporate.

Some of the regulated items the inspectors will check include: distance of project from property lines, handrail heights, stair construction, connection methods, footing sizes and depths,

material being used, plumbing, electrical and mechanical requirements and neighborhood zoning regulations.

Site Plan

Creating a site plan, or detailed layout of the project on the property, is important when incorporating a new addition to an existing landscape. A site plan allows you to view in advance the effect a new structure will have when finished. It is important to conceptualize how the new addition blends in with property lines, utilities, other structures, permanent mature plants, land contours and roads. You also need to be certain of the visibility of the new structure from vantage points both outside and within your property lines. In addition, a site plan may be required by local building officials.

Tools Checklist

If you are an experienced do-it-yourselfer, you probably have most of the tools needed for any of the projects in this book. If this is your first project, compare the tools you have on hand to the list below. Most are available at rental shops, so you can have "the right tool for the job" without spending a lot of extra money right at first.

Gather together the tools you will need for your project before you begin construction. This simple rule is as important as having your building materials and lumber on site in the needed sizes and quantity before you start. The frustration and aggravation you eliminate will be well worth the time it takes to get organized before you begin.

Your basic tool list should include:

Brushes & rollers to apply finishes	Power drill & screwdriver
Carpenter's level	Power jigsaw
Carpenter's square	Shovel
Chalk line	Socket set
Chisel	Tape measure
Circular saw	Tool belt
Framing angle	Line level
Hammer	Nail set
Handsaw	Wheelbarrow (to
Plumb bob	move materials & to mix concrete)

Selecting Lumber

Each project in this book has a list of lumber and other building materials required. You will need to determine and select the type of wood you want to use. Many wood species are used for outdoor structures. For most structures that may be used as living spaces, you'll want to choose a good construction-grade wood. For other structures such as sheds or gazebos you might decide on some of the more common woods, such as redwood, Western Red Cedar, Douglas Fir, Spruce, Southern Yellow Pine, Northern Pine and Ponderosa Pine. Enlist the help of a local lumber supplier when making your final decisions.

> *Lumber that is in contact with, or even in close proximity to, the ground must be decay-resistant.*

One of the primary considerations in selecting the correct lumber for your project is to prevent the base structure from decaying. For this reason, lumber that is in contact with, or even in close proximity to, the ground must be decay-resistant. Select a resistant species or treat your lumber with a preservative before using it in your building or project.

You might want to select pressure-treated wood, which is available from most lumber dealers and home centers. In pressure-treated wood, preservatives or fire-retardant chemicals are forced into the fibers of the lumber to protect and prolong its durability. Although pressure-treated wood seems an obvious choice, some precautions and decisions about its use are warranted. Because of the chemicals used in its treatment, pressure-treated wood should not be used if it will come into direct contact with drinking water or food for humans or animals. Further precautions include: do not use boards with a visible chemical residue; wear a mask and goggles when sawing treated wood; do not burn treated wood; and sweep up and safely dispose of all saw-

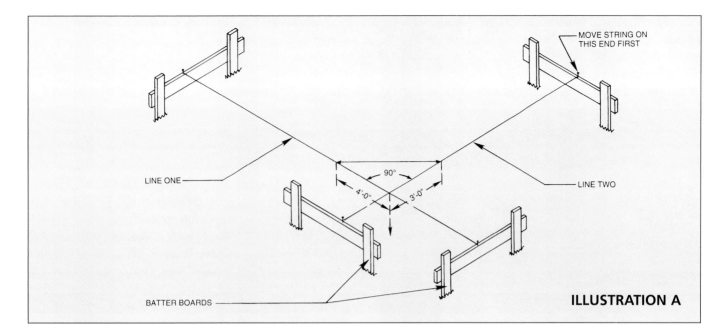

LINE ONE

90°

4'-0"   3'-0"

LINE TWO

BATTER BOARDS

ILLUSTRATION A

dust and wood scraps. Check with your lumber supplier for additional restrictions and precautions.

Choose a lumber dealer you can rely on to assist you with wood selection—one who will be familiar with the lumber commonly used in your area for garages and other outdoor buildings. Be sure what you want is available locally. If you desire a wood type that is not normally in stock in your part of the country, you'll pay much more to acquire it.

SITE PREPARATION

At last, it's time to begin! You've selected the site according to your observations and site plan; you've obtained complete project plans; you've secured all permits; and you've gathered together all code-approved materials and required tools. Now, to help assure success, follow these important steps so construction will proceed quickly and without too many hitches.

Drainage: This is an important word to remember when you begin construction. Water must drain away from the foundation or it will pool on structural supports, eventually rotting and weakening them. And, water saturated soil beneath footings may not remain firm enough to support the structure.

The easiest way to supply drainage is to slope the ground away from your structure so water will run off naturally. If the ground does not slope naturally, dig a drainage channel or channels to carry water away. Notice where water runoff flows naturally and install trenches there.

If runoff is light, dig trenches about 1 foot deep and line with 1 to 2 inches of gravel. If possible, direct the runoff downhill into irrigation wells for trees and shrubs. This form of water harvesting has dual benefits: it takes care of excess water and it supplies plants with needed moisture.

If runoff is heavy, further engineering will be required, such as laying perforated pipe, or lining the trenches with concrete. Consult with an architect or engineer to see if these or additional methods are required to handle heavy runoff.

Remove weeds and turf: Getting weeds out of the way before you begin to build makes construction easier. Hoe or pull

> **Water must drain away from the foundation or it will pool on structural supports, eventually weakening them.**

out weeds in small areas. In larger areas, a small cultivator can be used to turn over the soil. Keep cultivation shallow or weed seeds will be brought up to the soil surface to germinate.

To prevent future weed growth, lay down heavy black plastic sheeting (at least 6 mils thick). Newly available "fabric mulch" is also good for this purpose. It prevents weed growth, yet allows water to pass through and soak into the soil, which results in less runoff downgrade. Cover the sheeting or mulch with about 2 inches of pea gravel to hold it in place.

PROJECT LAYOUT

A simple surveying procedure allows you to be sure your project will be built square, with true 90-degree angles. Batter boards are used to square the starting corner of your project. This corner could be the outside wall of the foundation or the center point of your first post. The first step is to construct a right triangle using the "3-4-5 Method" described below. (Actually, any multiple of 3-4-5, such as 6-8-10, or 12-16-20 will work—the larger the better.)

The 3-4-5 Method

Using stakes and string, run a line (Line One) parallel to what you have determined will be the front of your project. Install batter boards as shown in Illustration A (see below) and attach string. Be sure the batter boards are far enough apart to build your project between. Install a second set of batter boards perpendicular to Line One and attach Line Two. Using a length of string

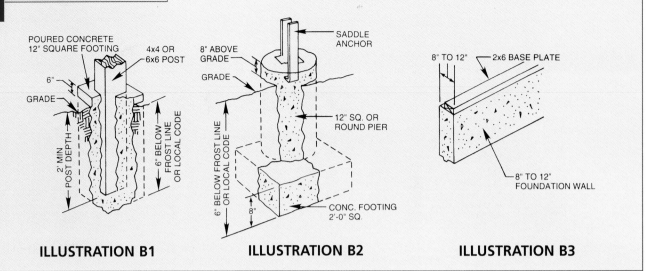

ILLUSTRATION B1   **ILLUSTRATION B2**   **ILLUSTRATION B3**

or a measuring tape, measure 4 feet along Line One from the point where it intersects Line Two. Mark that point with a piece of string that will slide. Measure 3 feet along Line Two from the Line One/Line Two intersection point and mark it with a piece of string that will slide. Next, measure 3 feet along Line Two from the Line One/Line Two intersection and mark it in the same manner. Now, measure the distance across from the string you tied to Line One to the string on Line Two. The corner is exactly square when this distance is five feet.

Adjust the string on the far end of Line Two and slide the string on Line One until the measurements equal the correct ratio. Double-check the accuracy by placing a carpenter's square in the corner. This process will establish a point with a perfect 90-degree angle from which to begin building your project. Regardless of where the point is it will become the main reference point for the entire project.

FOUNDATIONS, FOOTINGS AND PIERS

A poor foundation can ruin even the best project. Illustration B presents three options for a foundation, using piers and a poured concrete wall on a footer. Other methods include a concrete block foundation wall, or even placing your structure directly on precast concrete piers.

Local codes vary in requirements for footing sizes and depths. If you are in an area where the ground freezes, footings must be placed at the code-recommended depth below the soil level. Be sure to check the codes in your area before installing the footings for your project.

Piers, footings and foundations are the base of any project. Piers are formed from concrete, either pre-cast or "pour-your-own." To pour your own, either build your own forms from lumber, or use the ready-made forms-of-wax-impregnated cardboard, available in cylinder or block shapes, at local home-improvement or lumber supply stores.

To build a foundation wall, you must first pour the footing. A trench is dug below the frost line to the required dimensions of the footing. The footing is usually 8" to 10" deep by 16" to 20" wide. Once the concrete has set, build

> *All connectors should be of the highest quality 16- to 18-gauge hot-dipped galvanized steel.*

the foundation wall forms on top of the footing. The concrete is poured between the forms. An optional method is to set a block foundation wall on top of the footing. Pre-cast piers are available in various sizes and with drift-pin connections. These can be set on grade or sunken into the ground, depending on the type you select.

ATTACH PROJECT TO FOUNDATION

Whether your project is sitting on posts or a foundation wall, all wood within 12 inches of the soil should be treated as required by most codes. Illustrations B1 and B2 show the two most common ways to attach a post to a footing or pier. By setting metal connectors in poured concrete you will create a strong connection less susceptible to wood rot than simply sinking a post in concrete. All connectors should be of the highest quality 16- to 18-gauge hot-dipped galvanized steel. Ensure that all nails, bolts, nuts and other fittings exposed to the elements are also of galvanized steel.

Illustration B3 shows the base plate on the top of the trench footing secured with anchor bolts.

Many additional foundation options are available, such as slab flooring with anchor ties, block walls and others. The one you need will be indicated in the detailed set of plans for each project.

Leveling Post Height

If you are pouring a foundation wall or laying block, the top should be perfectly level for placing the sill plate. Since posts set in or on top of a footing or pier may vary in height, follow these guidelines. Use a post 6 inches longer than needed to allow for variations. After the concrete has set, string a level

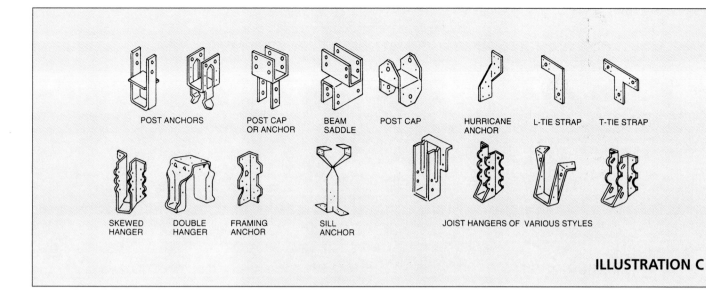

POST ANCHORS   POST CAP OR ANCHOR   BEAM SADDLE   POST CAP   HURRICANE ANCHOR   L-TIE STRAP   T-TIE STRAP

SKEWED HANGER   DOUBLE HANGER   FRAMING ANCHOR   SILL ANCHOR   JOIST HANGERS OF VARIOUS STYLES

ILLUSTRATION C

line to find the top of the post height needed for your project. Level the posts and cut to the same height prior to attaching floor joists or beams.

Making Framing Connections

Joists, rafters and even sill plate connections can be made stronger by using manufactured metal framing devices. Illustration C shows a variety of connectors and their applications. Other connectors are available which are easy to install and provide a strong connection.

FLOOR CONSTRUCTION

Slab foundations are used for the flooring in most of the structures in this book. If you are building a gazebo or other structure using decking, the joists may attach to the posts or beams with the decking extended to the edge. It may also be modified for railings or columns, as shown in Illustration D.

> *Structures in this book which have an upper level are constructed using conventional western platform techniques.*

Second-Floor Construction

In general, structures in this book which have an upper level are constructed using conventional western platform techniques. Additional bracing

can be provided with blocking or cross-bridging. "Blocking" uses boards the same dimension as the joists, placed between the joists for added support. "Cross-bridging" uses 2x3s or 2x4s placed in an X pattern between joists for added support. If blocking boards are cut precisely to size before joists are installed, they can serve as a measure to ensure correct spacing between joists. Stagger the blocking pattern to make it easier to install.

Be sure all joists are installed at the same level. Because the actual project flooring goes on top of the joists, they must be the same height or the surface of the floor will be uneven. To check, place a line over the joists and pull it tight. It will be easy to tell which joists are too high or too low and need to be adjusted.

Splicing Joists

Joists, like beams, must be spliced when they do not span the entire distance between beams. Splice only above a beam to ensure needed support. Use a wood or metal cleat, or overlap the joist at the beam. Extend the joint at least 8 or more inches beyond the sides of each beam to increase the strength of the junction and to allow room for the splice.

> *Joists, like beams, must be spliced when they do not span the entire distance between beams.*

If the joist spans over 8 feet, apply a cross-brace or blocking to prevent twisting. The longer the distance, the more likely the joist is to twist. If the floor span of your project is 8 feet or less, the end headers normally provide enough support so that cross-

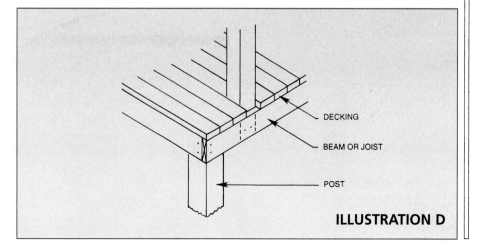

DECKING

BEAM OR JOIST

POST

ILLUSTRATION D

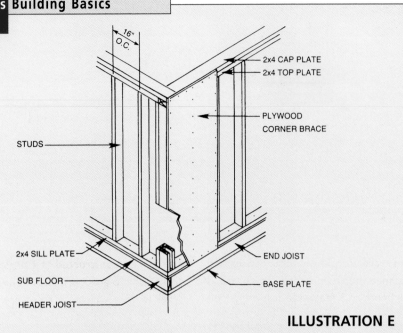

16"
O.C.

2x4 CAP PLATE
2x4 TOP PLATE

PLYWOOD
CORNER BRACE

STUDS

2x4 SILL PLATE

SUB FLOOR

HEADER JOIST

END JOIST

BASE PLATE

ILLUSTRATION E

degree angle, or metal "T" bracing, but using plywood is the easiest and fastest method. For small structures with ⅝" T-111 siding, or equal, this could also serve as the needed corner bracing and is sufficient for most codes.

Prior to starting the wall construction, be sure to verify all rough opening sizes for doors, windows, etc. All headers above the doors and windows are constructed of 2x material, which is really 1½" thick. With two 2x6s or two 2x8s with a ½" plywood spacer, you can build a header to support almost any window or door span for the projects in this book, except garage door headers, in which glue laminated beams are used.

ROOF FRAMING

Up to the cap plate or top plate, the method of construction depends on the type of framing system used. Above the cap plate, the method of construction depends mainly on the style of the roof indicated for the structure.

> *The two most common roof styles are the gable and the hip.*

Two structures built from identical plans can look considerably different when only the style of the roof is changed. The two most common roof

bracing is not required. Use blocking for added support for joists that are 2x4, 2x6, or 2x8, but for joists that are 2x10 or larger, install wood or metal cross bracing.

STANDARD WALL CONSTRUCTION

In platform framing, exterior walls and interior partitions have a single 2x4-plate (2x6 when studs are 2x6s) that rests on the subfloor. This is called the bottom or sole plate. The top of the walls have a doubled plate called the top plate, or cap plate, that supports ceiling joists, and, in most cases, roof rafters. The walls of a structure usually are built lying flat on the subfloor, then raised into position in one section. Wall studs are also normally placed 16" on center, but if 2x6 studs are used, then 24" on center may be acceptable.

There are a number of ways to construct the corner post. The method shown in Illustration E is one of the most common. Also shown is a sheet of exterior plywood at the corner. This is used as corner bracing. There are other methods, such as a 2x4 notched at a 45-

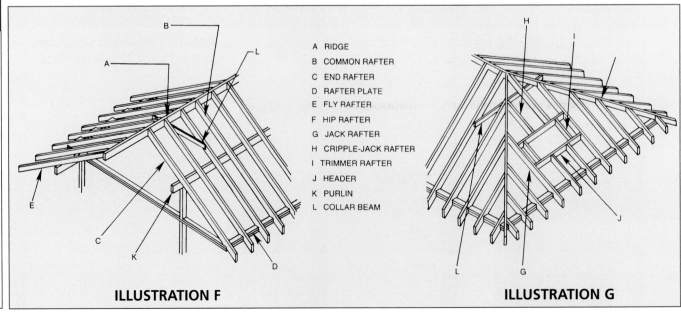

A RIDGE
B COMMON RAFTER
C END RAFTER
D RAFTER PLATE
E FLY RAFTER
F HIP RAFTER
G JACK RAFTER
H CRIPPLE-JACK RAFTER
I TRIMMER RAFTER
J HEADER
K PURLIN
L COLLAR BEAM

ILLUSTRATION F

ILLUSTRATION G

styles are the gable (Illustration F) and the hip (Illustration G), however, other styles are also used, such as a shed roof or gambrel roof, plus variations and combinations of each style.

There are five roof-framing terms you should know, which are used in calculating rafter length: span, rise, run, pitch, and pitch line, as shown in Illustration H. To construct a roof you will need to use a rafter square, available from local suppliers. Get either a metal angle or a triangular square. The least expensive model is a plastic triangular square. It comes with instructions on how to use it to measure rafters, cut angles, and cut "the bird's mouth," which is the part that sits on the wall cap plate. Because cutting the roof rafters is probably the most difficult task involved in building a garden structure, the rafter square is the most useful tool you can have.

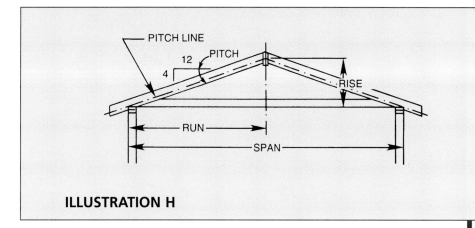

ILLUSTRATION H

STAIRS AND STEPS

Many projects require stairs and steps to provide exits to ground level or to upper-level living quarters. Stairs are composed of the tread, the surface you walk on, and the riser, the vertical distance between steps. Stairs are a minimum of 3 feet wide. It is important that you retain a constant riser-to-tread ratio. This ensures an equal distance between steps to avoid missteps and stumbles. A common riser-to-tread ratio is 6:12, which can be built by using two 2x6 treads and a 2x6 riser. For example, if the width of the tread is 12 inches, the next step should "rise" 6 inches.

The supports to which the steps are attached are called stair stringers or carriage, usually built from 2x12s. Steps can also be constructed as a single step from floor to ground, or from one floor level to another. Some steps are constructed as a separate level, a kind of continuous step, from one floor level to another. Illustration I shows the options for stringers and treads, plus a chart indicating standard tread-riser ratios.

INSULATION

If you are going to heat or cool your structure, you may want to insulate the walls and ceiling. If so, the normal wall insulation is R-19 in cold climates, with R-38 for the ceiling. R-values vary according to climate, so check with your local supplier for the requirements in your area.

RECOMMENDED READING

Residential Framing, by William P. Spence, Sterling Publishing Co.

Graphic Guide to Frame Construction, by Rob Thallon, The Taunton Press.

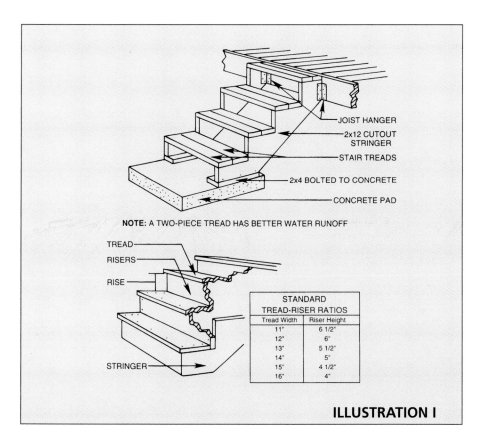

NOTE: A TWO-PIECE TREAD HAS BETTER WATER RUNOFF

STANDARD TREAD-RISER RATIOS	
Tread Width	Riser Height
11"	6 1/2"
12"	6"
13"	5 1/2"
14"	5"
15"	4 1/2"
16"	4"

ILLUSTRATION I

GLOSSARY

Anchor bolt: A device for connecting wood members to concrete or masonry.

Blocking: Used for added support for floor joists and to prevent twisting.

Balustrade: A complete handrail assembly. Includes rails, balusters, subrails and fillets.

Batter board: Simple wooden forms used early in construction to mark the corners of the structure and the height of foundation walls.

Beam: A horizontal framing member of wood or steel, no less than 5 inches thick and at least 2 inches wider than it is thick.

Board: Any piece of lumber more than 1 inch wide, but less than 2 inches wider in thickness.

Common rafter: Any of several identical structural members of a roof that run at right angles to walls and end at right angles to main roof framing members.

Concrete: A mixture of cement, sand, gravel and water.

Cross-bridging: Diagonal wood braces that form an "X" between floor joists.

Drip edge: A strip of metal used to protect the edges of a roof structure from water damage.

Drywall: A method of covering wall and ceiling surfaces with dry materials, rather than wet materials such as plaster. Refers primarily to the application of gypsum wallboard, also called drywall.

Edge joist: The outer joist of a floor or ceiling system that runs parallel to other joists. See header joist.

Foundation: The part of a building that rests on a footing and supports all of the structure above it.

Frame: The wood skeleton of a building. Also called framing.

Header: Any structural wood member used across the ends of an opening to support the cut ends of shortened framing members in a floor, wall or roof.

Header joist: The outer joist of a floor or ceiling system that runs across other joists. See edge joist.

Joist: A horizontal structural member that, together with other similar members, supports a floor or ceiling system.

O.C.: Abbreviation for On Centers, a measurement from one center line to the next, usually of structural members.

Ridgeboard: The horizontal board at the ridge to which the top ends of rafters are attached. Also called a ridge beam or ridge pole.

Plan HPT280076 page 78

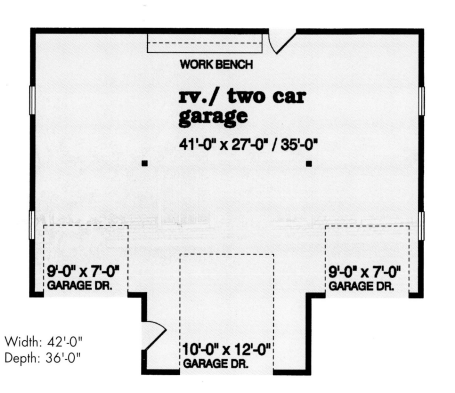

WORK BENCH

rv./ two car garage

41'-0" x 27'-0" / 35'-0"

9'-0" x 7'-0"
GARAGE DR.

9'-0" x 7'-0"
GARAGE DR.

10'-0" x 12'-0"
GARAGE DR.

Width: 42'-0"
Depth: 36'-0"

PLAN HPT280001

For the family with lots of "toys" this garage offers the perfect storage options with 1,320 square feet of space. The center section has an extra wide and tall door to accommodate campers and RVs, while each of the two side sections can hold an auto, a boat, or any combination. The center door measures 10' x 12' and each side door is 9' x 7'. An entry door in the center section allows easy access to all vehicles. There's even room for a handy workbench at the back of the garage.

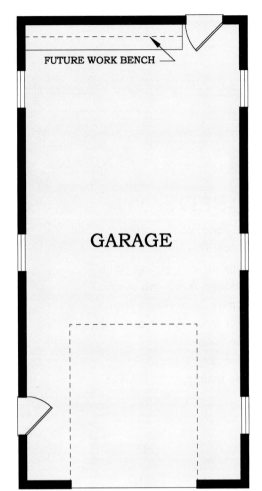

FUTURE WORK BENCH

GARAGE

Width: 18'-0"
Depth: 36'-0"

G
PLAN HPT280002

When you want to protect your home-away-from-home in style, this garage plan can provide the solution. A full 648 square feet of space is available with this plan. Natural light is directed through two sets of windows, to illuminate the top and bottom of the RV when it's safely tucked inside the garage. A side-entry door allows access to the interior of the garage without raising the main garage door.

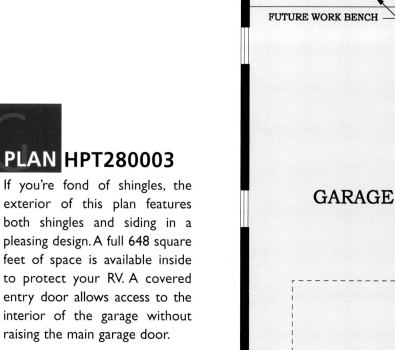

FUTURE WORK BENCH →

GARAGE

Width: 18'-0"
Depth: 36'-0"

PLAN HPT280003

If you're fond of shingles, the exterior of this plan features both shingles and siding in a pleasing design. A full 648 square feet of space is available inside to protect your RV. A covered entry door allows access to the interior of the garage without raising the main garage door.

G **PLAN** HPT280004

This garage plan includes room for both the RV and the car—or maybe the RV and a workshop! Enter the 984 square feet of space via a side-entry door or one of the car or RV entries. Plenty of room inside the garage will allow you to maintain your vehicle even during inclement weather.

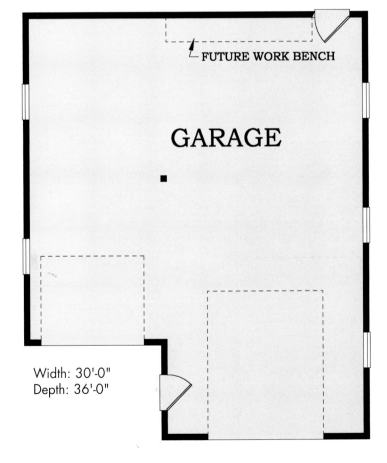

FUTURE WORK BENCH

GARAGE

Width: 30'-0"
Depth: 36'-0"

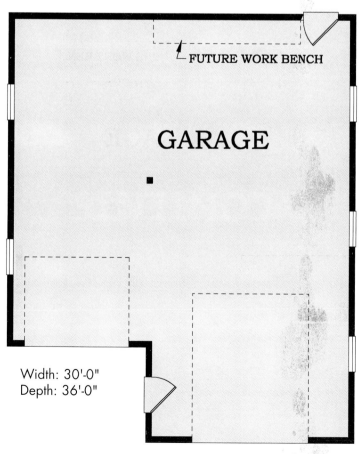

FUTURE WORK BENCH

GARAGE

Width: 30'-0"
Depth: 36'-0"

PLAN HPT280005

Inside and out, this combination RV and car garage pleases the eye. The exterior features wood shingles, vertical siding and a decorative border, all under an L-shaped gable roof. Inside, 984 square feet allows for plenty of storage. A side-entry door provides access to the interior without opening the larger vehicle doors.

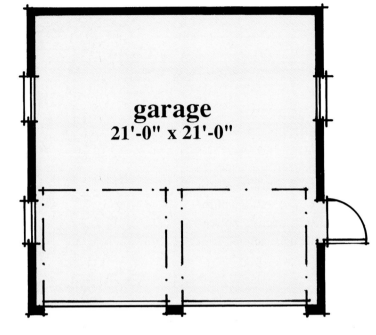

PLAN HPT280006

Vented dormers and a high-pitched insulated metal roof dress up this two-car, 484-square-foot garage with quaint details that blend beautifully with any traditional neighborhood home. With three windows and a side entry, this garage is convenient and well lit.

garage
21'-0" x 21'-0"

Width: 22'-0"
Depth: 22'-0"

PLAN HPT280007

Nestled at the back of your property or located adjacent to the main house, this spacious, 294-square-foot, hip-roof garage provides shelter and security for one, two or three vehicles. A raised curb, stretching the entire 36'-8" width, can be used to accommodate a workbench for small projects. Or, because of the proximity and access to the backyard through an exterior door, the curb area is a natural for a potting bench. The addition of brick and masonry planters at each outside corner of the garage adds architectural interest and softens the lines of this straightforward design.

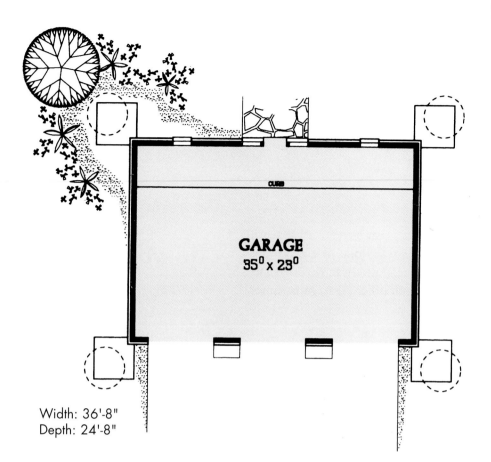

GARAGE
35⁰ x 23⁰

Width: 36'-8"
Depth: 24'-8"

PLAN HPT280008

Situated at the back of your property or located alongside the main house, this spacious 704-square-foot garage will protect three cars and have room to spare. Imagine a workshop in one of the car bays. A gable sets off the hipped roof of this structure.

three car garage

31'-4 x 21'-4

Width: 32'-0"
Depth: 22'-0"

PLAN HPT280009

Square panels adorn the garage door of this two-car garage. A hipped roof protects the top of the 440-square-foot interior, while horizontal siding shields the sides. A gable dresses up the side above one of the two windows, which provide a cross breeze when the garage door is closed. A side-entry door near the rear provides access to both storage and automobiles.

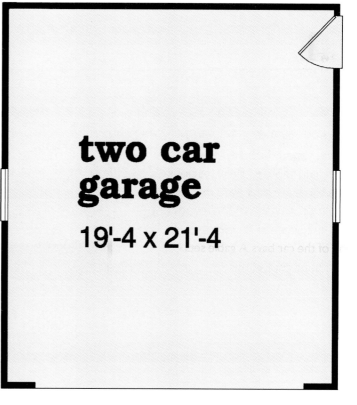

two car garage

19'-4 x 21'-4

Width: 20'-0"
Depth: 22'-0"

PLAN HPT280010

Three 9' x 7' garage doors convert this 768-square-foot area equally well to private or commercial use. Vary the selection of siding and door jambs on this wide-gable roof structure to blend with the style of your home. For use on a commercial site, choose the options for electrical outlets in each bay area. Plenty of room is provided along the 32' back wall for a workbench and a storage area. A pre-hung steel door at the back side wall allows convenient entry and exit.

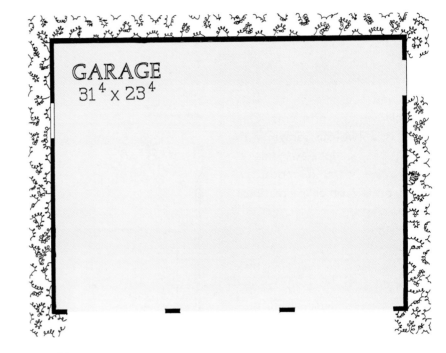

GARAGE
31^4 x 23^4

Width: 32'-0"
Depth: 24'-0"

PLAN HPT280011

Have more vehicles than space to store them? This clever garage design provides 1,008 square feet and the answer to your vehicle storage problems. One side is a two-car garage, with plenty of space for both vehicles. The other side accommodates a boat or any other recreational vehicle easily—and is extra long for those luxury "toys." A gable roof and windows on three sides pretties up the exterior and makes this out building a good match for your main residence.

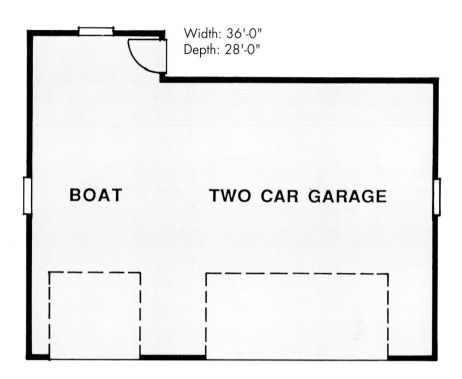

Width: 36'-0"
Depth: 28'-0"

BOAT   TWO CAR GARAGE

PLAN HPT280012

Is it a garage? Is it a workshop? The answer is both. You can put this 900-square-foot area to work however it suits you best—and modify the exterior to match your house. Providing space enough for three cars is only the first benefit. Convert the third parking bay to an optional work pit—perfect for the devoted mechanic's do-it-yourself car maintenance. A generous work area adjacent to the parking bay allows space for a counter, air compressor, welders and other tool-time essentials. The back wall storage area includes optional cabinets and a wash sink, with handy side-door access for bringing the mower and other yard equipment in out of the weather. Three different exterior elevations are available.

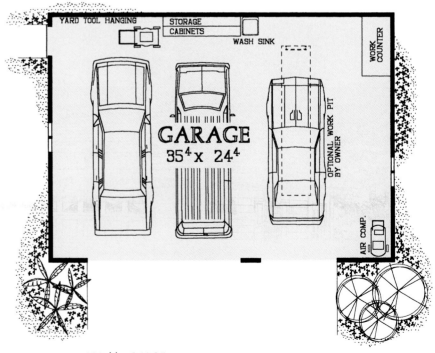

YARD TOOL HANGING
STORAGE CABINETS
WASH SINK
WORK COUNTER

GARAGE
35⁴ x 24⁴

OPTIONAL WORK PIT BY OWNER

AIR COMP.

Width: 36'-0"
Depth: 25'-0"

Plan HPT280013

Plan HPT280014

PLAN HPT280015

With 600 square feet of room, this two-car garage also accommodates adequate storage areas for tools, yard and gardening equipment, and recycling and trash bins. A 16'x7' garage door provides safe passage for vehicles, and an exterior door at the back of the side wall offers easy access to the storage areas. Three different exterior elevations are available, ensuring a perfect blend of style with the main house structure.

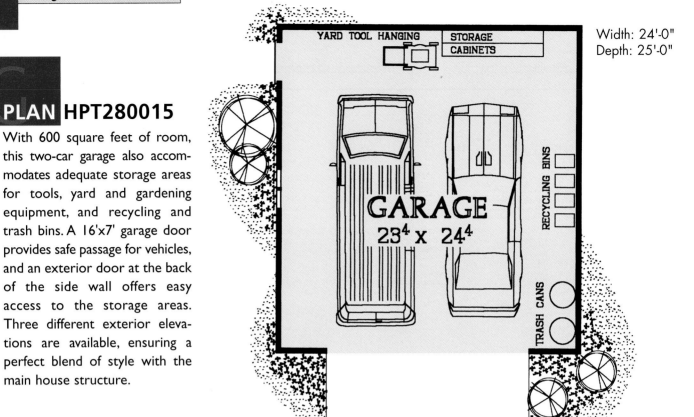

Width: 24'-0"
Depth: 25'-0"

Plan HPT280017

Plan HPT280016

PLAN HPT280018

A good choice for chilly climates, the steep pitch of this hip-roof design will stop snow build-up cold. The solid brick construction topped with decorative shingles offers 552 square feet of space to get two cars safely in out of the weather. Natural light enters through a double-hung window in the side wall, and side entry is provided by a pre-hung door near the front...just a short dash to the house.

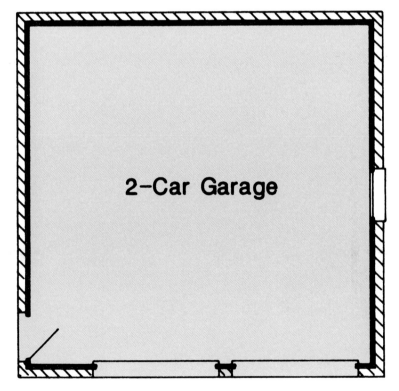

2-Car Garage

Width: 24'-0"
Depth: 23'-0"

GARAGE
23^5 x 23^5

PLAN HPT280019

Intended to be versatile, this 576-square-foot, two-car garage with deep eaves and wide-panel siding offers a generous work area. Enter by either of the 9' x 7' garage doors, or by the pre-hung steel door in the back side wall. Natural light is provided through translucent panels in the garage doors. Conveniently placed electrical outlets in each parking bay and two in the back wall increase the versatility of this multi-use structure.

Width: 24'-0"
Depth: 24'-0"

Width: 24'-0"
Depth: 24'-0"

GARAGE
23⁵ x 23⁵

PLAN HPT280020

With the same basic specs as the plans on page 29, this version, provides a garage with slightly smaller overall dimensions, 576 square feet of space and horizontal siding. Plan HPT280022 offers 768 square feet of usable area whereas Plan HPT280021 features 784 square feet of room and both plans feature vertical siding. Overall, the deep eaves and siding offer a no-nonsense approach two-car garage with a generous work area. Enter by either of the 9' x 7' garage doors, or by the pre-hung steel door in the back side wall. Natural light is provided through translucent panels in the garage doors. Conveniently placed electrical outlets in each parking bay and two in the back wall increase the versatility of this multi-use structure.

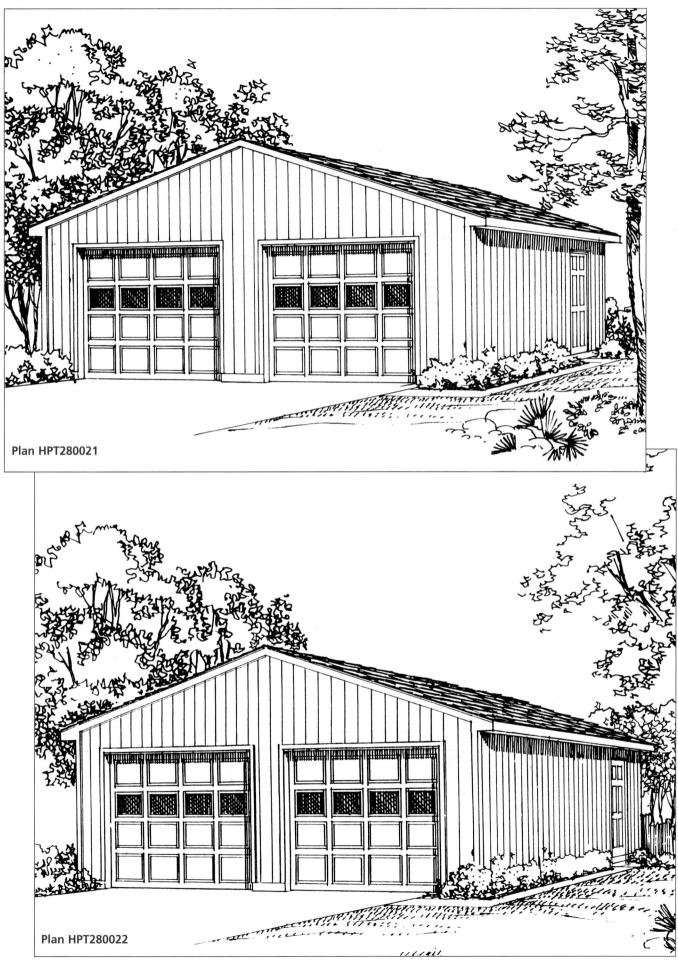

Plan HPT280021

Plan HPT280022

Width: 22'-0"
Depth: 22'-0"

 PLAN HPT280023

A wide-gable roofline provides a generous overhang on all sides of this compact garage with a single 16' x 7' garage door flanked by exterior lights. The 484-square-foot floor plan allows space for a workbench and storage area along the back wall. A double-hung window along the side wall provides natural light, while an exterior door in the back wall gives easy access to the work and storage area.

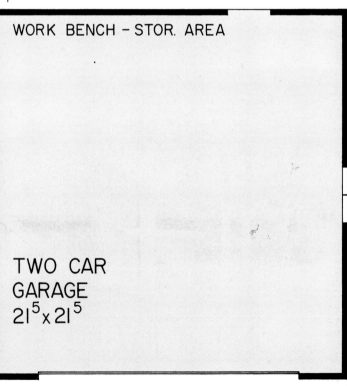

WORK BENCH – STOR. AREA

TWO CAR
GARAGE
$21^5 \times 21^5$

C PLAN HPT280024

Store your car and your bike or your car and your motorcycle, plus have room left over for a workbench and generous storage areas. The 385-square-foot floor plan has a curbed work area at the back with 14 feet of garage storage. Additional storage is provided in a second area—4' x 11'-5"—adjacent to the garage door. Both storage areas are easy to reach through an exterior side door. Natural light enters through a double-hung window in the 24' side wall.

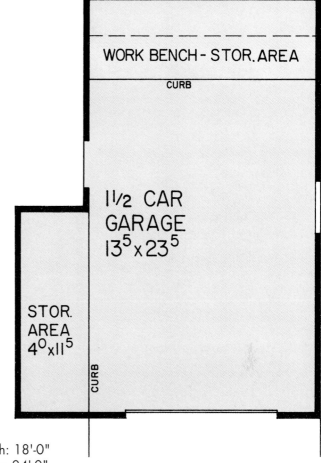

WORK BENCH - STOR. AREA

CURB

$1\frac{1}{2}$ CAR GARAGE $13^5 \times 23^5$

STOR. AREA $4^0 \times 11^5$

CURB

Width: 18'-0"
Depth: 24'-0"

Width: 24'-0"
Depth: 24'-0"

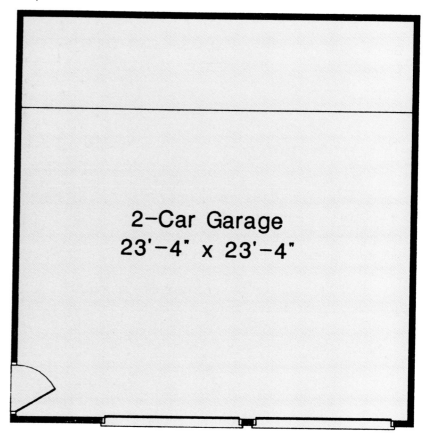

2-Car Garage
23'-4" x 23'-4"

PLAN HPT280025

A neat facade, this compact two-car garage will make the most of the 545 square feet of space available, plus add a decorative accent to your main house. The gabled roof can support a mixed design of shingles to complement your choice of siding and garage doors. An easy-access exterior door in the side wall and a curb along the back for storage or work space add to this structure's usefulness.

PLAN HPT280026

Go Creative! Much more than protection for two cars, this nifty little 552-square-foot number is full of surprises. The gable roof sports an intersecting overhang to form an eight-foot shaded area supported by three brick-and-pillar columns with decorative arched trim. A double-hung sash window front and center, complete with shutters, adds natural light and lots of appeal. A one-more-for-good-measure triangle of trim above the window, and a side door for easy access make this plan all but irresistible. Additional light is provided through clear panels on the garage doors and a window in the back wall.

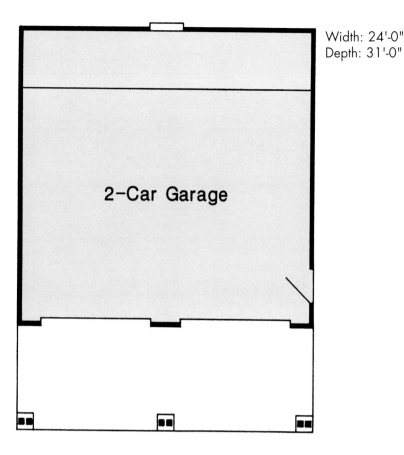

Width: 24'-0"
Depth: 31'-0"

2-Car Garage

PLAN HPT280027

Square panels and rounded, individual garage doors give this two-car, 528-square-foot garage a charming character. A rear-entry door allows access to stored items within the garage. Natural light is provided through clear panels on the garage doors and a window on the side wall.

Width: 24'-0"
Depth: 22'-0"

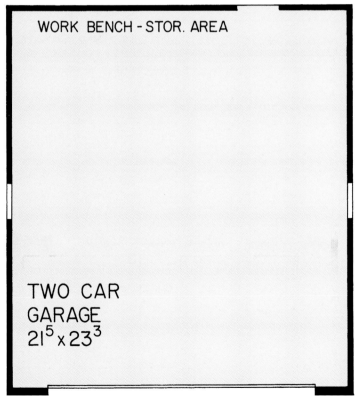

WORK BENCH - STOR. AREA

TWO CAR
GARAGE
$21^5 \times 23^3$

Width: 22'-0"
Depth: 24'-0"

PLAN HPT280028

Notched corners on the steeply pitched roof of this wood-shingled garage enhance the wrought-iron exterior lights on each side of the 17' x 7' door. The 528-square-foot area provides plenty of room for two cars, plus a workbench and storage area. Opposing double-hung windows in the side walls are neatly framed with shutters, and louvered vents in the gable peak allow for controlled air flow.

Width: 22'-0"
Depth: 24'-0"

WORK BENCH - STOR. AREA

TWO CAR
GARAGE
21^5 x 23^3

G

PLAN HPT280029

The high-pitched roof of this free-standing, 528-square-foot garage shelters two cars, plus room enough for a workbench and welcome extra storage. Slotted shutters on the opposing double-hung windows are repeated in miniature to flank the louvered vent at the peak of the roofline. Wide wood trim around the recessed-pattern garage door creates a clean, uncluttered line.

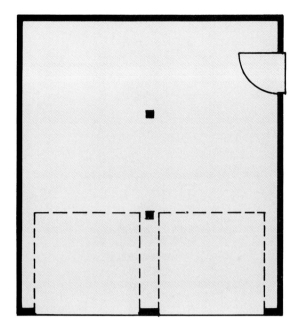

Width: 20'-0"
Depth: 22'-0"

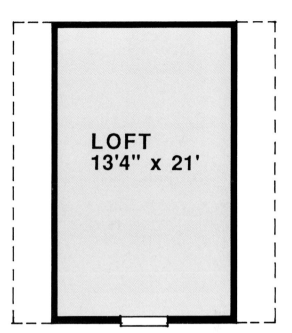

LOFT
13'4" x 21'

PLAN HPT280030

If you've played with the idea that your car is your pony, this fanciful garage will add to the mystique. With a barn-like roof and a decorative hay-bale door above the two individual garage doors, this plan will add to any country setting. Horizontal siding enhances the 440-square-foot design. The loft adds 284 square feet of space. Natural light is provided through clear panels on the garage doors.

PLAN HPT280031

This functional single-car garage will suit either a large or small lot. The Adjustable plan includes 16' x 20' with 320 square feet of usable area, whereas the shed style on page 39 includes 16' x 24' with 384 square feet of space. Choose a garage door style with clear panels to provide natural light. Optional electrical service in the center of the parking bay adds versatility to the many uses of this sturdy structure. A wide, gable roofline and vertical siding allow this design to blend easily with many traditional and contemporary house styles. Access to the storage in the back is through a pre-hung exterior door in the side wall.

Plan HPT280032

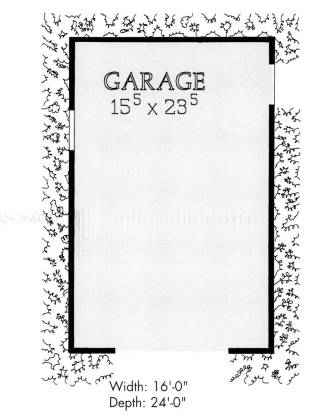

GARAGE
15⁵ x 23⁵

Width: 16'-0"
Depth: 24'-0"

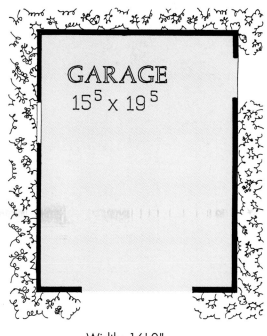

GARAGE
15⁵ x 19⁵

Width: 16'-0"
Depth: 20'-0"

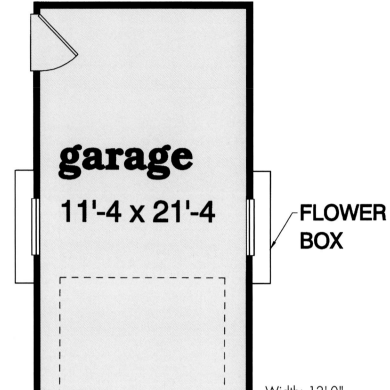

garage
11'-4 x 21'-4

FLOWER BOX

Width: 12'-0"
Depth: 22'-0"

G PLAN HPT280033

When a single-car garage will do, this 264-square-foot plan will provide a winning look. Flower boxes adorn both windows, creating a welcoming appearance. Horizontal siding adds a polished look. A charming hipped roof caps this simple plan.

PLAN HPT280034

The hipped roof, horizontal siding and box-bay window of this charming single-car garage will enhance any yard. Square solid and clear panels on the garage door as well as the entry door—with the clear panels allowing additional light to the interior—add texture to the exterior. This garage design includes dimensions of 16' x 20' and 320 square feet of usable area for storage and car care.

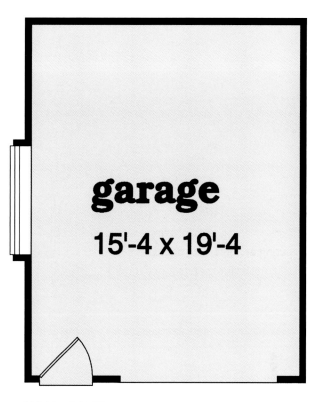

garage

15'-4 x 19'-4

Width: 16'-0"
Depth: 20'-0"

G PLAN HPT280035

This 16' x 20' one-car garage plan is perfect to set back into a heavy foliage area. Enter the 320-square-foot interior through the multi-paneled car door or the entry door to the left. Horizontal siding and a gabled roof protect all your stored valuables. A side window and clear panels on the garage door illuminate the interior with natural light.

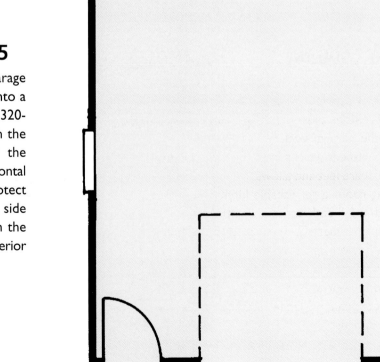

Width: 16'-0"
Depth: 20'-0"

PLAN HPT280036

Almost too grand to be a mere garage, this design provides enough space for three vehicles, plus a handy work area at the garage level. The second-floor apartment weighs in at a sizable 1,167 square feet and allows for a large living room, a serviceable kitchen, a bedroom with a full bath and even a study. Use it for frequent guests, a mother-in-law, college student or even as a home office. The exterior of this garage fits nicely with almost any style of home, but will work especially well with European, Southwestern or Mediterranean designs.

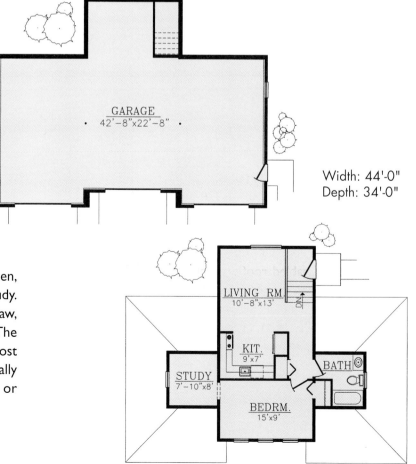

GARAGE
· 42'-8"x22'-8" ·

Width: 44'-0"
Depth: 34'-0"

LIVING RM.
10'-8"x13'

KIT.
9'x7'

STUDY
7'-10"x8'

BATH

BEDRM.
15'x9'

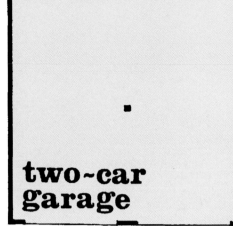

two-car
garage

Width: 27'-6"
Depth: 22'-0"

PLAN HPT280037

This handy two-car garage has charm galore, plus additional space on the second level for guests or in-laws, or to be used as a rental apartment. It's a 484 square-foot one-bedroom apartment, with living and dining space, complete kitchen, and full bath. The bedroom contains a box-bay window and wall closet. A deck off the living room is reached via sliding glass doors. The dining room, kitchen, and bath all feature windows. Access this apartment by a stairway to the left of the double garage.

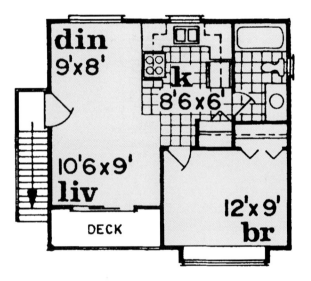

din
9'x8'

k
8'6x6'

10'6x9'
liv

DECK

12'x9'
br

PLAN HPT280038

This Tudor-style garage is more than just a handy place to park two cars—it also features a large 247-square-foot workshop area with a skylight and wrapping countertops. Disappearing stairs in both the garage section and the workshop section gain access to attic space, which may be finished into a studio or used for storage as needed. The outside could be modified to suit any style of home, using different materials for a different look.

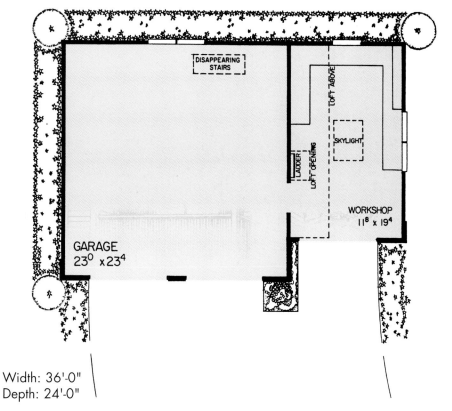

DISAPPEARING STAIRS

LOFT ABOVE

LADDER

LOFT OPENING

SKYLIGHT

GARAGE
23⁰ x23⁴

WORKSHOP
11⁸ x 19⁴

Width: 36'-0"
Depth: 24'-0"

PLAN HPT280039

This two-car garage offers a farmhouse exterior with a bonus! A one-bedroom apartment with a spacious vaulted living room, full kitchen, separate bath and a rear deck takes up the 512-square-foot second floor. The downstairs entry offers a coat closet and garage and laundry access.

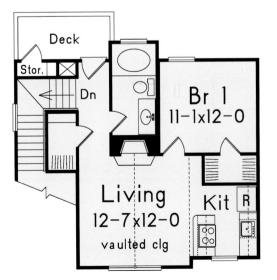

Deck

Stor.

Dn

Br 1
11-1x12-0

Living
12-7x12-0
vaulted clg

Kit R

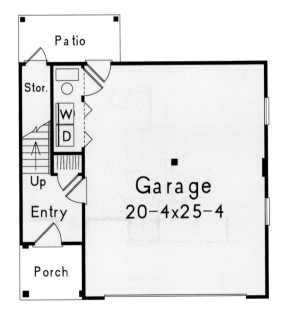

Patio

Stor.

W
D

Up

Entry

Porch

Garage
20-4x25-4

Width: 28'-0"
Depth: 26'-0"

46

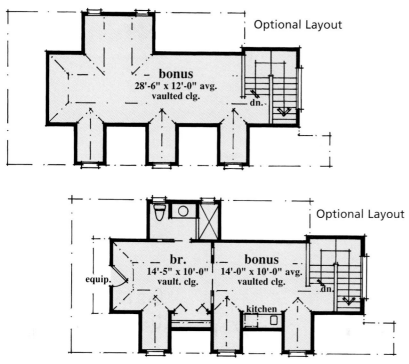

Optional Layout

bonus
28'-6" x 12'-0" avg.
vaulted clg.

dn.

Optional Layout

equip.

br.
14'-5" x 10'-0"
vault. clg.

bonus
14'-0" x 10'-0" avg.
vaulted clg.

dn.

kitchen

Width: 47'-6"
Depth: 22'-0"

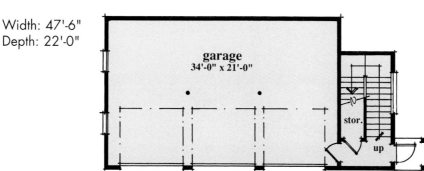

garage
34'-0" x 21'-0"

stor.

up

PLAN HPT280040

A portico-style entry is a warm welcome to this detached three-car garage, styled to complement many of the neighborhood designs. Bonus space above offers 497 square feet of additional living area or a recreation room. With a morning kitchen, full bath, vaulted ceiling and three dormered windows, Option A may be developed as a comfortable guest suite or a charming artist's studio. The entry vestibule provides ample storage space as well as a wrapping stair to the bonus level.

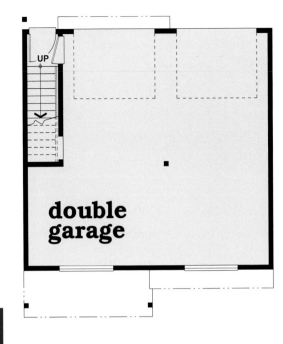

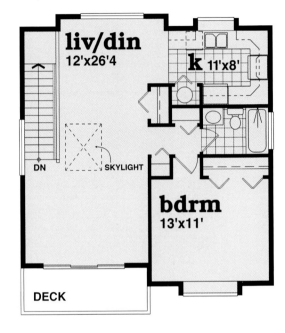

Width: 28'-0"
Depth: 31'-4"

liv/din
12'x26'4

k 11'x8'

DN SKYLIGHT

bdrm
13'x11'

DECK

double
garage

UP

PLAN HPT280041

This cottage garage sports siding and both a porch and upper-level deck. A two-car garage completes the first level while a spacious 773-square-foot apartment rounds out the second level. A large living and dining space enjoys a skylight and access to the deck. The U-shaped kitchen features all the amenities for small-scale living. A full bath and a bedroom with wall closet and bumped-out bay window finish up the apartment.

PLAN HPT280042

Traditional good looks with open gables, siding and a covered porch conceal the impressive and efficient interior of this two-car garage and apartment combination. A private entry accesses a stairway to the 819-square-foot second floor. The large living room has a wonderful deck and is open to the dining area. The kitchen is a perfect fit, featuring a window sink for gazing. Two bedrooms—one a master suite with a vaulted ceiling—and a full bath complete this plan.

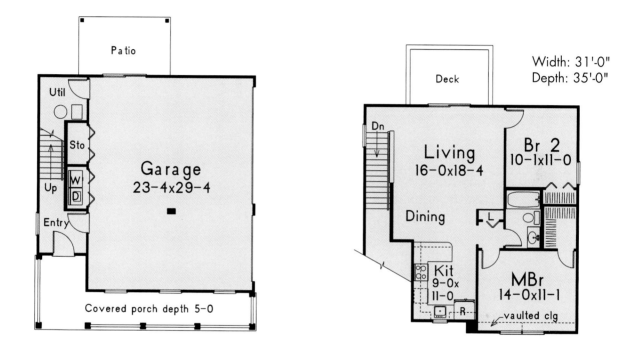

Width: 31'-0"
Depth: 35'-0"

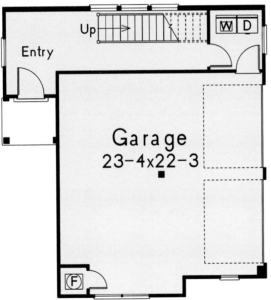

Up

Entry

W D

Garage
23-4x22-3

F

Width: 30'-0"
Depth: 32'-0"

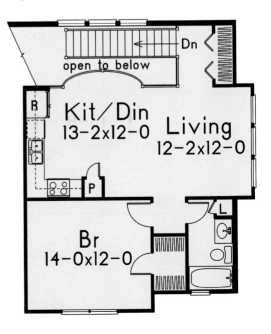

Dn

open to below

R

Kit/Din
13-2x12-0

Living
12-2x12-0

P

L

Br
14-0x12-0

PLAN HPT280043

Strong angles give this Northwestern design a contemporary appeal. The first-floor entry boasts a laundry closet with access to the two-car garage. The 664-square-foot second level features a living room with plenty of windows to take advantage of the views. An open kitchen and dining area enjoys an overlook to the entry floor. A full hall bath and bedroom with walk-in closet round out this plan.

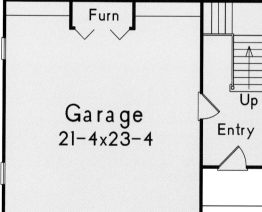

Garage
21-4x23-4

Furn

Up

Entry

Width: 29'-0"
Depth: 24'-0"

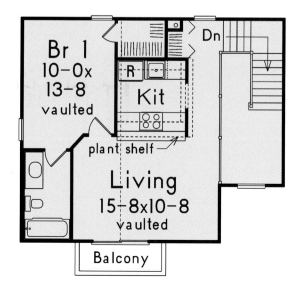

Br 1
10-0x
13-8
vaulted

Kit

Dn

plant shelf

Living
15-8x10-8
vaulted

Balcony

PLAN HPT280044

A fantastic display of wood siding makes this two-car garage/apartment a great place for guests. Upstairs, the 528-square-foot living space includes a spacious vaulted living room with a balcony, a very efficient galley-style kitchen and plenty of closet storage. A full bath can be found in the bedroom which enjoys a walk-in closet and vaulted ceiling.

PLAN HPT280045

This shed-style plan with clerestory windows will provide that additional space an existing house with a growing family needs. Imagine adding not only a garage but an office, studio or game room to your home. The loft area adds 320 square feet of living area to this two-car garage.

two-car garage

LOFT

Width: 28'-0"
Depth: 27'-0"

PLAN HPT280046

A loft apartment sits conveniently above a two-car garage—perfect as an addition to an existing home, or as a home of its own. The garage area is roomy enough for two cars and storage space. The second floor has **468** square feet of living space. Light will pour into the studio apartment through numerous windows, protected by large eaves. A full kitchen and bath complete the plan.

Width: 28'-0"
Depth: 26'-0"

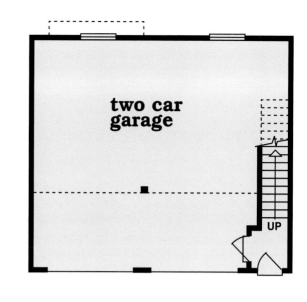

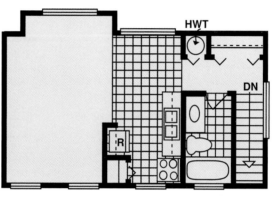

G PLAN HPT280047

This two-car, side-entry garage with 701 square feet of cozy living space upstairs is perfect for in-law suites or a guest cottage. The sheltered front porch adds charm while camoflaging the garage facade. The apartment features a generously sized great room, plus an efficient kitchen, full bath and bedroom. Natural light pours into the great room through a long row of clerestory windows. The garage features more than enough room for two cars and ample garden equipment storage.

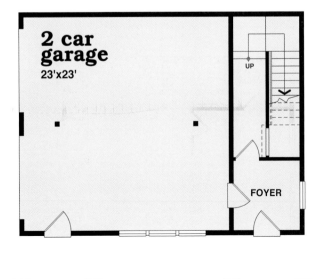

2 car garage
23'x23'

UP

FOYER

ST

L

F

HWT

br
11'x11'4

DN

k
9'8x11'7

R

great room
23'x11'4

Width: 32'-0"
Depth: 30'-8"

C PLAN HPT280048

Perfect for a guest apartment, or as an income possibility, this fine Craftsman carriage house will look good in any neighborhood. With rafter tails, a shed dormer, a gabled porch roof and a stone-and-siding facade, the Craftsman style is highly evident. A two-car garage shares space with a laundry room and a half bath, while the 679-square-foot main living space is upstairs. Plenty of storage can be found at the first landing of the stairs. The living room is open to the stairwell, and is adjacent to the petite yet efficient kitchen. The bedroom features a walk-in closet.

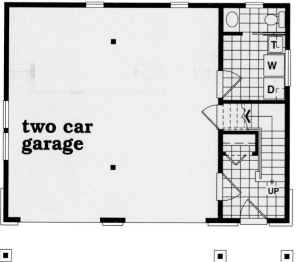

two car garage

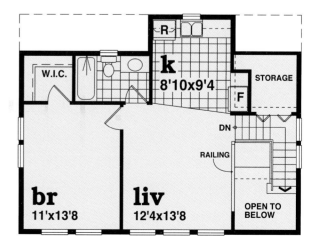

W.I.C.

k
8'10x9'4

STORAGE

DN

RAILING

br
11'x13'8

liv
12'4x13'8

OPEN TO BELOW

UP

Width: 32'-10"
Depth: 28'-4"

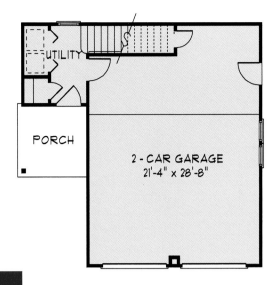

UTILITY

2 - CAR GARAGE
21'-4" x 28'-8"

PORCH

Width: 30'-6"
Depth: 29'-4"

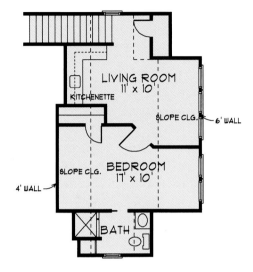

LIVING ROOM
11' x 10'

KITCHENETTE

SLOPE CLG.

6' WALL

SLOPE CLG.

BEDROOM
17' x 10'

4' WALL

BATH

PLAN HPT280049

Approach from either of the sides and this deceptive design looks like a guest cottage. Approach from the driveway and it is a two-car garage. The attractive modified-gable roof covers 553 square feet of living area on the second floor. Interior stairs lead from the laundry area off the two-car garage to the living room and the bedroom—both with sloped ceilings.

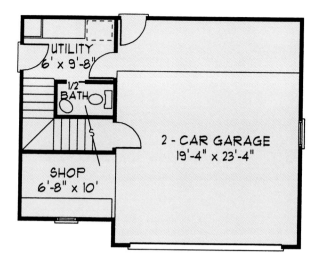

UTILITY
6' x 9'-8"

1/2
BATH

SHOP
6'-8" x 10'

2 - CAR GARAGE
19'-4" x 23'-4"

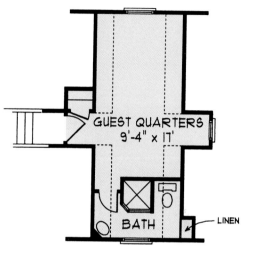

Width: 26'-8"
Depth: 24'-0"

GUEST QUARTERS
9'-4" x 17'

BATH

LINEN

PLAN HPT280050

The steeply pitched roof and perky single dormer make this floor plan look as though it is just waiting for Hansel and Gretel. Follow the bread crumbs to the 271-square-foot guest quarters on the second floor, where you'll find a bath with a shower and a linen closet. Downstairs there is space for two cars, a workshop, utility room and more—a half-bath tucked under the stairs. Double-hung, recessed, 6/6 sash windows add to the charming effect.

G
PLAN HPT280051

This well-thought-out floor plan is the perfect solution for a home office addition. A single 16'x7' garage door provides shelter for two cars, plus out-of-sight storage areas for yard and garden equipment, garbage cans and recycling bins. A four-column porch provides entry to the compact 321-square-foot apartment or office area. A mini-kitchen (or make this extra work space) and a bath with a shower provide added convenience. The bedroom at the back could also be used for additional storage. Different exterior elevations are available to better suit your home.

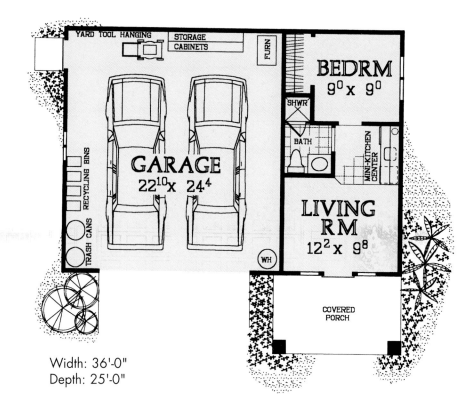

Width: 36'-0"
Depth: 25'-0"

Plan HPT280052

Plan HPT280053

PLAN HPT280054

An open gable featuring rafter accents and shingles promotes a Craftsman appeal. This two-car garage provides a workbench and plenty of work space. Stairs lead to a loft/studio—perfect for storage or as a hobby room.

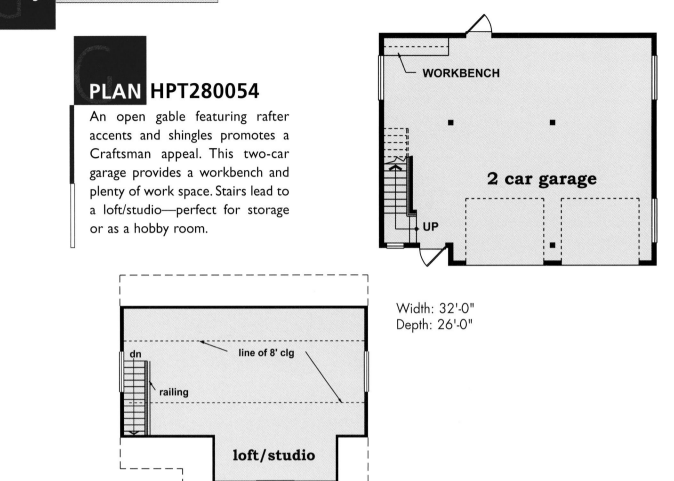

WORKBENCH

2 car garage

UP

Width: 32'-0"
Depth: 26'-0"

dn

line of 8' clg

railing

loft/studio

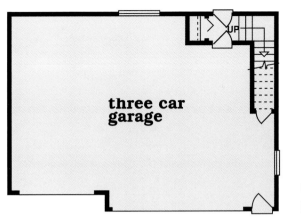

three car garage

Width: 34'-0"
Depth: 24'-0"

PLAN HPT280055

Shingles and Craftsman elements adorn the exterior of this appealing plan. A three-car garage fills the lower level, while a roomy apartment resides above. The 676 square feet of living space includes an L-shaped kitchen, light-filled living room, full bathroom and bedroom with a walk-in closet. Live in this charming home or use the space for rental income.

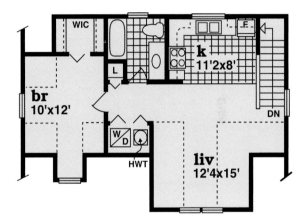

PLAN HPT280056

Shingles create a Northwestern feeling of woods and water. This 604-square-foot cottage would make a perfect retreat or guest home. A porch leads to the living room, which is open to the dining area and convenient kitchen. A full bath and bedroom complete the living accommodations. The two-car garage is set to the side.

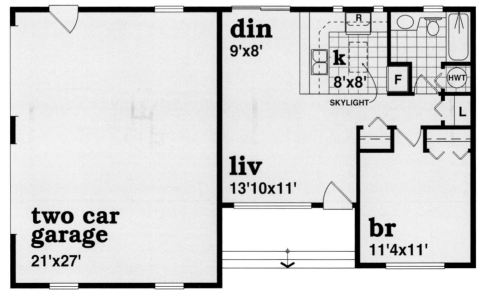

din
9'x8'

k
8'x8'

R

F

HWT

L

SKYLIGHT

liv
13'10x11'

two car garage
21'x27'

br
11'4x11'

Width: 48'-0"
Depth: 28'-0"

CPLAN HPT280057

This 794-square-foot design will house two members of the family fleet and includes a comfortable apartment—great for servant's quarters or tenants. This superb design includes a spacious floor plan with a bay window in the living room and skylit kitchen. Adding to the charm of this lovely one-bedroom home are the covered porch and central fireplace. A two-car garage occupies the left half of this design and includes a separate outdoor entrance.

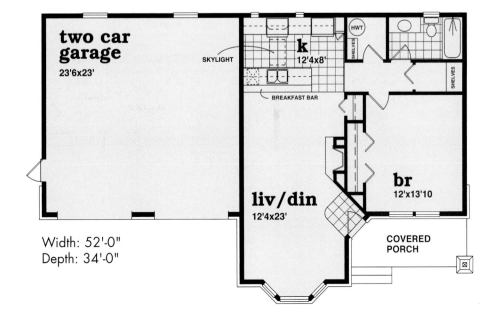

two car garage
23'6x23'

SKYLIGHT

HWT

SHELVES

SHELVES

k
12'4x8'

BREAKFAST BAR

liv/din
12'4x23'

br
12'x13'10

COVERED PORCH

Width: 52'-0"
Depth: 34'-0"

PLAN HPT280058

Greet your clients in the business side of this 306-square-foot multi-use structure. There's room enough for a reception/waiting room area in front with an impressive entryway through a columned porch. Decorative recessed windows flanking the door and two more in the side wall allow for plenty of natural light. In the back is ample space for an office with a storage closet and file space. Add a half bath for maximum convenience. These three facades will offer a perfect match to your home.

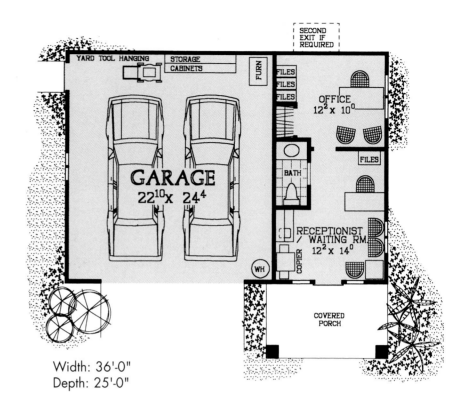

SECOND EXIT IF REQUIRED

YARD TOOL HANGING

STORAGE CABINETS

FURN

FILES
FILES
FILES

OFFICE
12² x 10⁰

FILES

BATH

GARAGE
22¹⁰ x 24⁴

RECEPTIONIST / WAITING RM.
12² x 14⁰

COPIER

WH

COVERED PORCH

Width: 36'-0"
Depth: 25'-0"

Plan HPT280059

Plan HPT280060

G PLAN HPT280061

Perfect for narrow lots, lakeside or otherwise, this darling little 582-square-foot Victorian-style cottage will serve as a wonderful retreat. The covered front porch leads to a bright living room and dining room area. A handy closet stores coats and outerwear. The U-shaped kitchen includes a windowed sink area. It directly accesses the bay-windowed dining area. A full bath with natural light is conveniently located. The bedroom, with lots of closet space and views from two sides, sits quietly at the rear of the plan. In the two-car garage, space exists for the placement of a washer and a dryer.

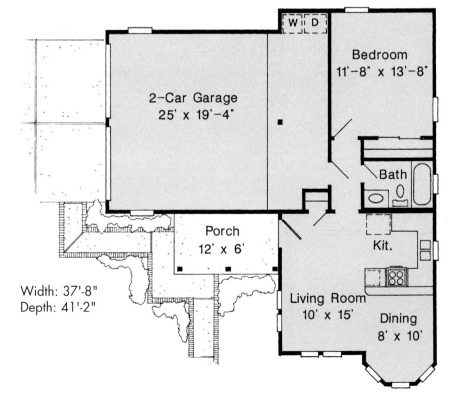

Width: 37'-8"
Depth: 41'-2"

2-Car Garage
25' x 19'-4"

W D
Bedroom
11'-8" x 13'-8"

Bath

Porch
12' x 6'

Kit.

Living Room
10' x 15'

Dining
8' x 10'

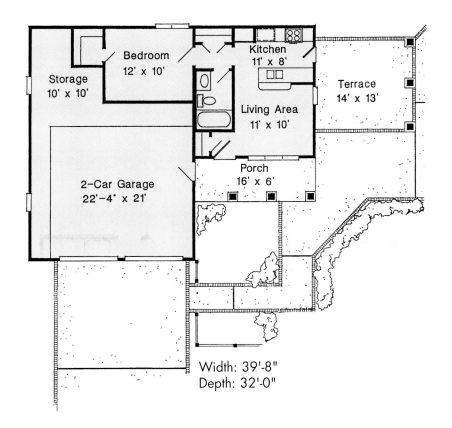

Bedroom
12' x 10'

Storage
10' x 10'

Kitchen
11' x 8'

Terrace
14' x 13'

Living Area
11' x 10'

2-Car Garage
22'-4" x 21'

Porch
16' x 6'

Width: 39'-8"
Depth: 32'-0"

PLAN HPT280062

This delightful 468-square-foot cottage features a columned porch and a side terrace—perfect for outdoor relaxation. Inside, the front-facing living room shares space with the efficiently patterned kitchen and includes a window overlooking the terrace. A coat closet sits right next to the front door. A large storage closet, between the kitchen and bath, will serve nicely as a pantry or a linen closet. The bedroom, with a large walk-in closet, enjoys peace and quiet at the rear of the plan. A step away, the full hall bath is also convenient to living areas. In the two-car garage, a large storage area accommodates recreational equipment.

C PLAN HPT280063

Behind what looks like just another garage door is just what you've always wanted—a fully equipped workshop. Accessed through an 8' x 7' garage door, or from an interior door within the garage itself, is 300 square feet of workshop area. It contains plenty of room for your favorite power tools, work table, storage cabinets, counter space and overhead racks for lumber. On the left side of this multi-use structure is a two-car garage with a 16' x 7' door. It allows space for yard and garden equipment, plus a convenient area for recycling bins and garbage cans. Varying facades make it easy to find a perfect match to your home.

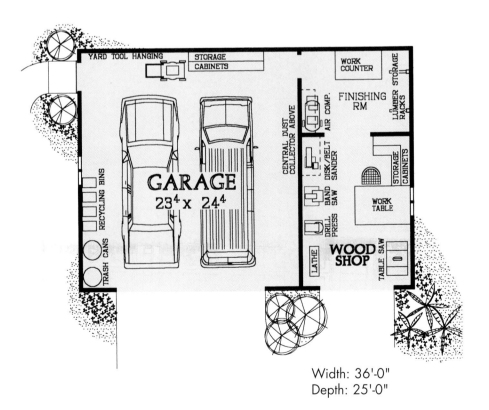

Width: 36'-0"
Depth: 25'-0"

Plan HPT280064

Plan HPT280065

G PLAN HPT280066

Two cars and a lap pool all fit inside this plan. If you don't happen to live where it's balmy year-round, tuck this figure eight-style pool in the 321 square feet to the right of the garage—all under one roof. Access to the pool is through an interior door in the garage, or from outside through its own separate door. Natural light pours into the pool area through four skylights— two on each slope of the roof. The garage has space for two cars with plenty of room left over for storing yard tools, garden equipment, and trash and recycling bins. For a different look, see our other facades.

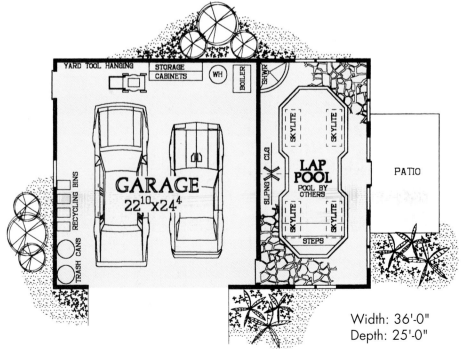

Width: 36'-0"
Depth: 25'-0"

Plan HPT280067

Plan HPT280068

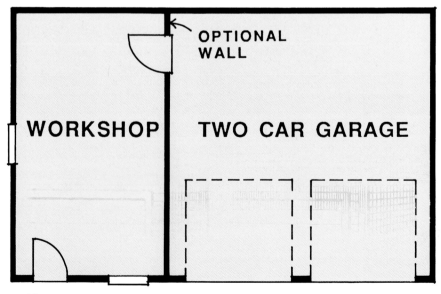

GPLAN HPT280069

This combination of workshop and two-car garage creates the ideal solution to additional space. A side-facing gable, siding and shutters really bring this design a down-home country feel. Use the workshop for storage or for gardening or woodworking hobbies. An outside entrance provides quick access or use the garage access.

OPTIONAL WALL

WORKSHOP

TWO CAR GARAGE

Width: 32'-0"
Depth: 20'-0"

PLAN HPT280070

Functional and attractive, this plan offers 516 square feet of extra living area, conveniently located above a roomy garage. The garage level protects up to three cars from the elements, while the loft area allows for storage space, an office, teen's apartment or an art studio in the future as your family expands.

three~car garage

LOFT

LINE OF 8' CEILING

Width: 34'-0"
Depth: 24'-0"

PLAN HPT280071

This brilliant garage design with twin dormers is full of surprises! Not only can this two-car garage provide shade from the sun, but the 588-square-foot second level can also serve as an in-law suite or a guest house. Upstairs, the living room connects to the kitchen and dining area. Just outside the bedroom—which features a walk-in closet—is a linen closet and a full bath. Don't miss the washer and dryer unit near the kitchen. Plan includes a slab foundation.

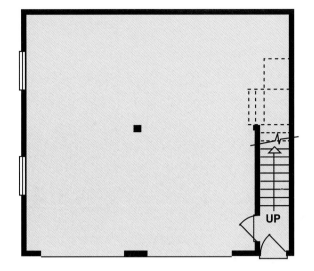

Width: 28'-0"
Depth: 24'-0"

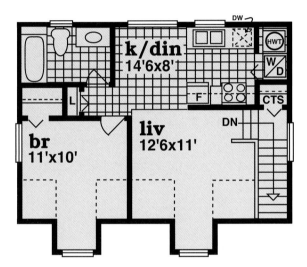

k/din 14'6x8'

HWT

W/D

CTS

L

F

DN

br 11'x10'

liv 12'6x11'

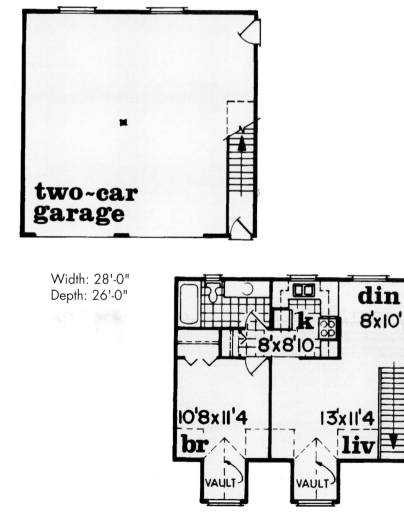

two-car garage

Width: 28'-0"
Depth: 26'-0"

din
8'x10'

k
8'x8'10

10'8x11'4

br

VAULT

13'x11'4

liv

VAULT

PLAN HPT280072

This two-car garage is more than a place to protect cars from bad weather. The 652-square-foot second story contains a living room adjacent to a dining area. A considerable amount of counter space is provided in the kitchen. In the bedroom a double-door closet and a vaulted ceiling add a touch of sophistication while just across the hall is a full bath.

PLAN HPT280073

Not a hideout for an errant spouse, this floor plan is a two-car garage, plus a 306-square-foot seven-pen kennel. Looking like a guest cottage from the outside, the area adjacent to the garage holds seven 4' x 5'-6" dog pens. A grooming area with deep sink and storage cabinets is in the rear near the back door which opens onto the dog run. A 16' x 7' door provides access to the garage for cars. Extra storage for yard and garden equipment as well as recycling and trash bins is also provided. Choose one of three facades for a different look.

Width: 36'-0"
Depth: 25'-0"

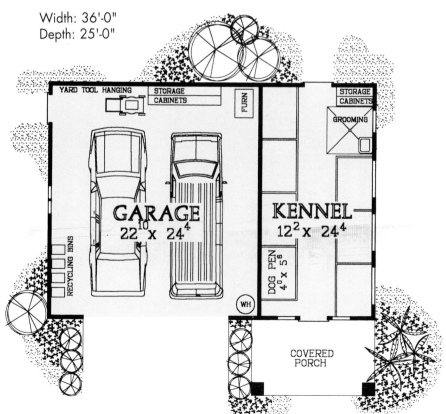

YARD TOOL HANGING   STORAGE CABINETS   FURN   STORAGE CABINETS

GROOMING

RECYCLING BINS

GARAGE
22^{10} x 24^4

KENNEL
12^2 x 24^4

DOG PEN
4^0 x 5^8

WH

COVERED PORCH

Plan HPT280075

Plan HPT280074

PLAN HPT280076

Attractive and functional, this impressive structure has room for three cars in the garage section and 670 square feet of living area—complete with kitchen, bathroom, bookshelves, and closet—to use as a studio or a hideaway loft for guests. The treatment of the steeply pitched gable roof is repeated in three gabled dormers, each with tall, narrow windows framed with shutters. Access to the second-floor loft area is via a railed exterior stairway which leads to a small landing with its own covered roof supported by wooden columns. The clipped corners of the trim around each of the three car bays lend country charm. Four wrought-iron coach lights complete the effect.

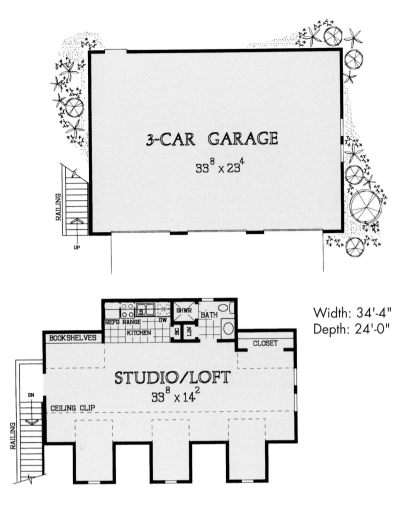

3-CAR GARAGE
$33^8 \times 23^4$

RAILING
UP

BOOKSHELVES
REFG RANGE
KITCHEN
DW
SHWR BATH
BC LIN
S
CLOSET

DN
CEILING CLIP
RAILING

STUDIO/LOFT
$33^8 \times 14^2$

Width: 34'-4"
Depth: 24'-0"

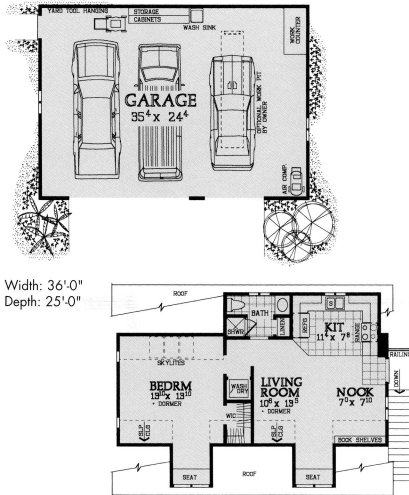

YARD TOOL HANGING
STORAGE CABINETS
WASH SINK
WORK COUNTER

GARAGE
35⁴ x 24⁴

OPTIONAL WORK PIT BY OWNER

AIR COMP.

Width: 36'-0"
Depth: 25'-0"

ROOF

BATH
LINEN
SHWR
REFG
KIT
11⁴ x 7⁸
RANGE
S

SKYLITES
RAILING

BEDRM
13¹⁰ x 13¹⁰
+ DORMER

WASH DRY

LIVING ROOM
10⁶ x 13⁵
+ DORMER

NOOK
7⁰ x 7¹⁰

DOWN

SLP CLG

WIC

SLP CLG

BOOK SHELVES

SEAT

ROOF

SEAT

RAILING

PLAN HPT280077

Decorative touches grace the exterior of this garage and guest cottage. The first-floor space holds room for a work pit or for three parking bays. The 690-square-foot second floor has a complete guest apartment. A fully equipped kitchen is on the right and ahead is a generous living room with built-in book-shelves and a tempting seat in the dormer window. A full bath with a shower and linen closet and laundry facilities add to the functional floor plan. A large bedroom features sloping ceilings and a welcome walk-in closet.

C PLAN HPT280078

Looking like anything but a three-car garage, this plan features a standard entry set back and accented with a porch with a covered roof—all supported by turned wooden posts. Interior stairs are placed between a generous utility room and separate workshop area, with an interior door leading from the stairwell into the garage and an exterior door leading outdoors from the back wall of the garage. Upstairs, 582 square feet of space greets you. A living room, bedroom with full bath, kitchen, storage and built-in bookshelves are included.

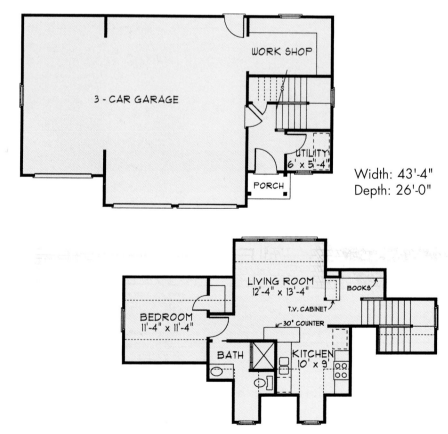

Width: 43'-4"
Depth: 26'-0"

C PLAN HPT280079

Corner quoins and two dormers with siding set a beautiful tone for this garage and guest cottage. The first-floor space holds room for a work pit or for three parking bays. The 690-square-foot second floor has a full apartment. The U-shaped kitchen on the right includes a window over the sink and ahead is a generous living room with built-in bookshelves and a tempting seat in the dormer window. A full bath with a shower and linen closet and laundry facilities add to the functional floor plan. A large bedroom features sloping ceilings and a welcome walk-in closet.

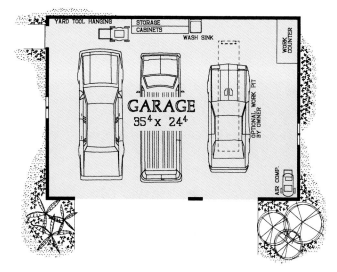

Width: 36'-0"
Depth: 25'-0"

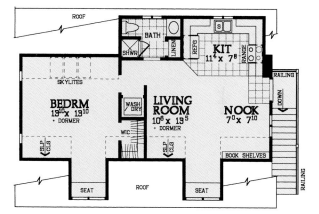

Width: 36'-0"
Depth: 25'-0"

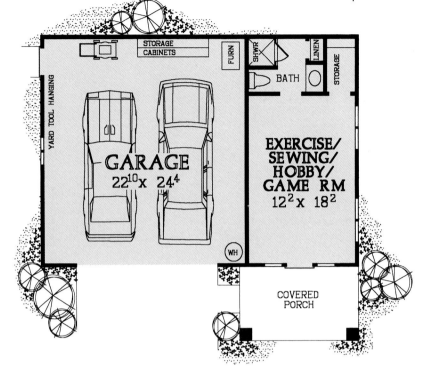

STORAGE CABINETS

FURN

SHWR

LINEN

STORAGE

BATH

YARD TOOL HANGING

GARAGE
22¹⁰ x 24⁴

EXERCISE/
SEWING/
HOBBY/
GAME RM
12² x 18²

WH

COVERED
PORCH

G PLAN HPT280080

The two-car garage area of this plan provides the basics, but the more than 300 square feet of optional-use area can be transformed into a game room, an exercise room or a separate space for sewing or other hobbies. Extra convenience is provided by a full bath with a shower and both linen and storage closets. Let your imagination take over when deciding which amenities you need to create a special workspace for your projects. In the garage, you'll find more than enough room for two cars, plus plenty of storage for yard and garden equipment, garbage cans and recycling bins. Two other facades offer a different look.

Plan HPT280081

Plan HPT280082

PLAN HPT280083

Winner of the Best Use of Space Award! This design provides protection for two cars, plus a 23'-4" x 13'-2" second-floor studio with three-quarter bath and storage in just 428 square feet. Entry to the second floor is via an exterior railed stairway with a roofed landing. Two gable-roofed dormers and two windows in the side wall provide plenty of light for arts and crafts and plenty of space for the college set to toss sleeping bags for a weekend visit. Access the garage through two wide doors, or through a standard entry door with a porch at the back wall.

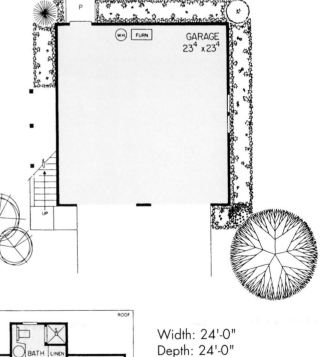

Width: 24'-0"
Depth: 24'-0"

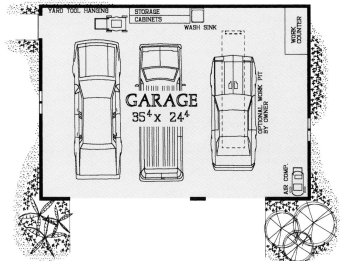

GARAGE
35⁴ x 24⁴

YARD TOOL HANGING
STORAGE CABINETS
WASH SINK
WORK COUNTER
OPTIONAL WORK PIT BY OWNER
AIR COMP.

Width: 36'-0"
Depth: 25'-0"

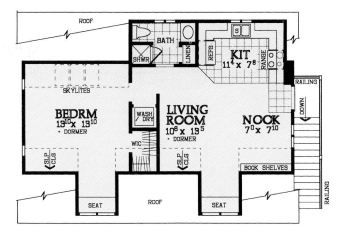

ROOF
BATH
SHWR
LINEN
REFG
RANGE
S
KIT
11⁴ x 7⁸
SKYLITES
BEDRM
13¹⁰ x 13¹⁰
+ DORMER
WASH DRY
LIVING ROOM
10⁶ x 13⁵
+ DORMER
NOOK
7⁰ x 7¹⁰
RAILING
DOWN
WIC
SLP CLG
SLP CLG
BOOK SHELVES
SEAT
ROOF
SEAT
RAILING

PLAN HPT280084

An array of shingles, millwork and decorative touches are incorporated in the exterior design of this garage and guest cottage. While the front exterior is highlighted by dormers with circle-head windows, a separate side stairway with a sheltered porch provides access to the second-floor guest apartment. Entry to the 690-square-foot living area is through an airy breakfast nook. A fully equipped kitchen is on the right, and ahead is a generous living room with built-in bookshelves and a tempting window seat in the dormer window. A full bath with a shower, linen closet and laundry facilities adds to the functional floor plan. A large bedroom features a sloped ceiling and a walk-in closet. An abundance of natural light enters through three skylights.

Width: 36'-0"
Depth: 25'-0"

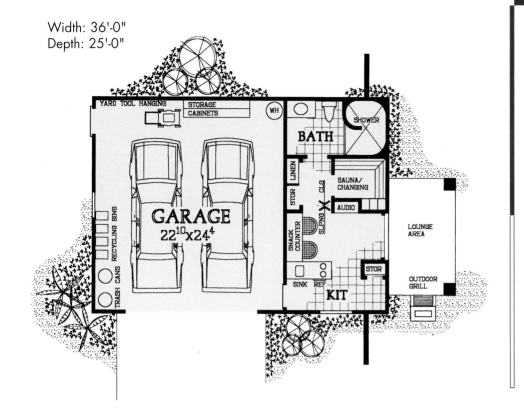

PLAN HPT280085

Locate this roomy structure near the pool and provide security for two cars, plus a spacious 321-square-foot bathhouse with a changing room and an outdoor patio/lounge area shaded by a generous roof extension. The garage area provides plenty of space to store yard and garden equipment. Natural light enters the interior through two skylights over the kitchen area. Built-in benches and countertops, plus storage and linen closets, offer lots of convenience. The kitchenette is cooled by a ceiling fan and French doors leading to the patio. Choose any of the three facades for a different look.

Plan HPT280087

Plan HPT280086

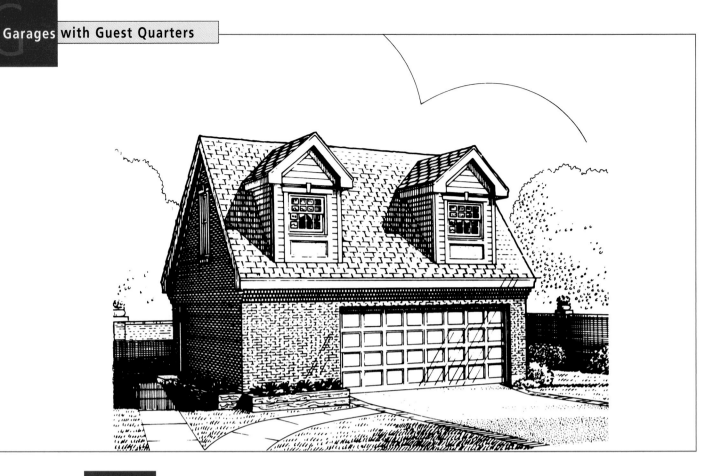

G PLAN HPT280088

This sturdy brick structure provides space in the garage for two cars and a snug little 364-square-foot apartment on the second floor. The second floor is accessed by an interior stairwell and features living accommodations for a guest or college-age child. Two gable-roofed dormers and two side windows provide natural light and fresh air throughout the living area, full bath and kitchenette.

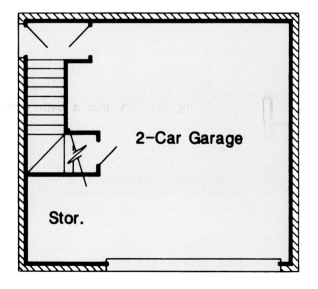

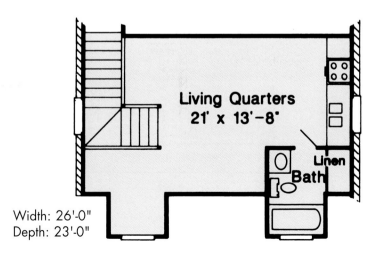

Width: 26'-0"
Depth: 23'-0"

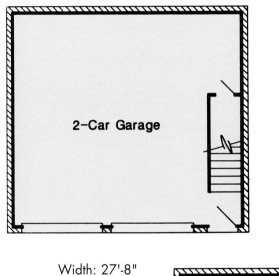

2-Car Garage

Width: 27'-8"
Depth: 25'-0"

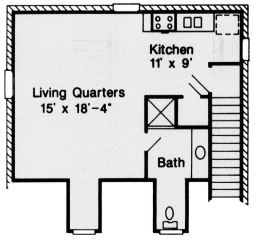

Kitchen
11' x 9'

Living Quarters
15' x 18'-4"

Bath

PLAN HPT280089

Designed to fit on Any Street, USA, this garage features a gambrel-style roofline with two pitch-roofed dormers containing double-hung sash windows. At ground level are two garage doors and an interior stairway leading to 525 square feet of living space upstairs. Full livability is found in the kitchen and the living quarters, plus a bath with shower. Windows in each of the side and back walls provide plenty of natural light and fresh air.

PLAN HPT280090

This two-car garage has an addition that serves multiple purposes—it can be a guest suite, a mother-in-law suite or a handy studio. It features a kitchenette and full bath, plus a large hall closet for storage. A stone patio graces the entry and provides a bit of outdoor space to enjoy. Contemporary in design, this garage/guest house may be finished to match any style of home.

Width: 61'-10"
Depth: 49'-8"

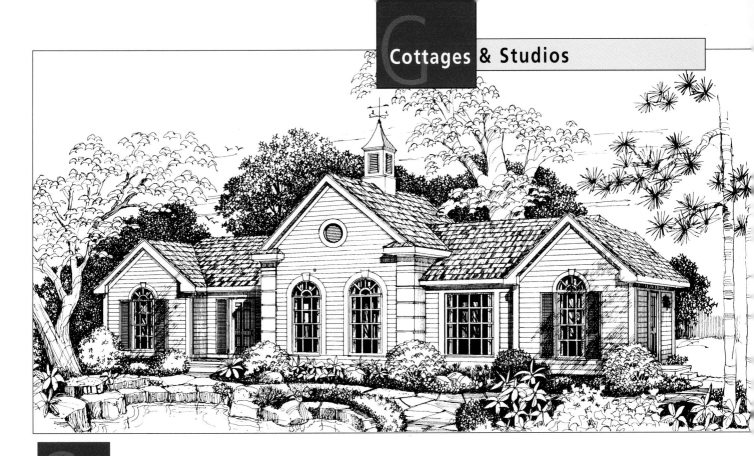

G PLAN HPT280091

Start small with this elegant, 324-square-foot, free-standing garden room. Use the space as a garden retreat for reading or music, or as an arts-and-crafts studio. Two tall, arched windows topped with fanlights grace three sides. A window and entry door flanked by narrow mock shutters are found in the front. The vented cupola and weathervane centered on the cedar shake roof add an air of rustic charm. To expand the living area an additional 664 square feet, extend the floor plan to each side. Add an entry foyer and full bath to one side of the existing structure and a breakfast nook with its own door to the garden on the other. Existing windows become doorways and, in one case, a window is replaced by an interior wall. To complete this outstanding expansion, add a bedroom and a kitchen with a pass-through window off the breakfast nook.

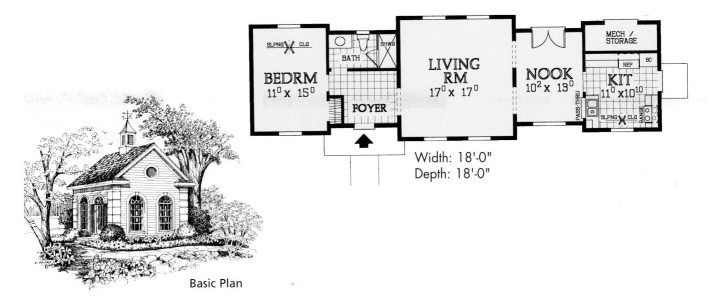

Basic Plan

Width: 18'-0"
Depth: 18'-0"

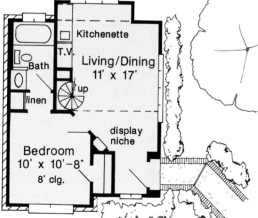

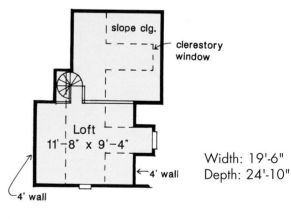

Width: 19'-6"
Depth: 24'-10"

PLAN HPT280092

This enchanting cottage is reminiscent of the guest quarter and gate houses of English country estates. Convert it to your own requirements with or without an optional 132-square-foot loft. The 10' x 10'-8" bedroom and large living/dining area, plus full bath and kitchenette, make this ideal for weekend guests or a quiet environment for your home office. Replace the shingle siding shown with stucco or horizontal siding to make this versatile design compatible with your main house.

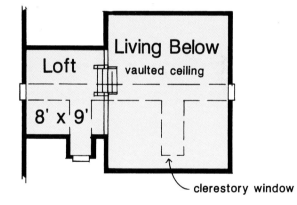

Width: 24'-0"
Depth: 36'-4"

Living Below
vaulted ceiling

Loft
8' x 9'

clerestory window

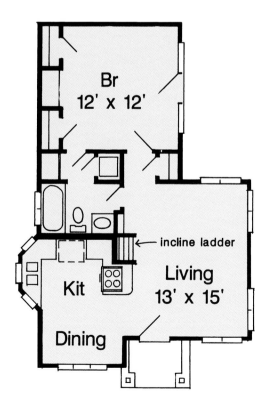

Br
12' x 12'

incline ladder

Living
13' x 15'

Kit

Dining

PLAN HPT280093

Enter this charming cottage through a covered porch with fieldstone walls. The design makes the most of the 627-square-foot, first-floor living area and provides additional space with a 90-square-foot optional loft. French doors on the 12' x 12' bedroom, a bow window in the kitchen and a vaulted ceiling with a clerestory dormer window bring the outdoors in. An incline ladder reaches the loft in this ideal getaway retreat.

2,80 X 3,10
9'-4" X 10'-4"

2,40 X 4,30
8'-0" X 14'-4"

3,00 X 7,20
10'-0" X 24'-0"

3,90 X 3,60
13'-0" X 12'-0"

Width: 22'-8"
Depth: 26'-8"

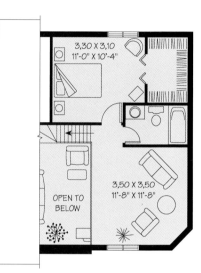

3,30 X 3,10
11'-0" X 10'-4"

3,50 X 3,50
11'-8" X 11'-8"

OPEN TO
BELOW

PLAN HPT280094

A stunning arch-top window sets off this charming European cottage. An angled entry and open planning allow a sense of spaciousness from the moment one enters the 976-square-foot home. A voluminous bedroom on this floor adjoins a full bath. The staircase leads to a second-floor mezzanine, which overlooks the living area and may be used as a study area or an extra bedroom. This home is designed with a basement foundation.

PLAN HPT280096

Capture elusive breezes upstairs or down through the matching sets of windows in this stately 763-square-foot two-story guest house or office suite. The grand exterior of this plan is complemented with brick quoins and keystone lintels, lending it a sophisticated air that will enhance any property. In the winter months, allow only sun in through the windows and enjoy the warmth and charm of a fireplace on both floors. A generous living area occupies the entire first floor. Upstairs you'll be at home—or at work—in a bedroom/office area, plus a bath with a tub.

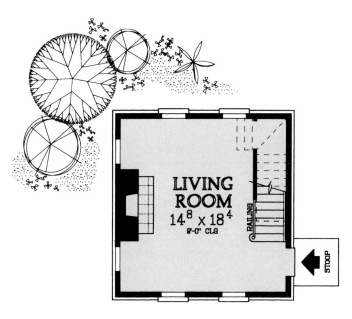

LIVING ROOM
14⁸ x 18⁴
9'-0" CLG

RAILING

STOOP

Width: 20'-0"
Depth: 20'-0"

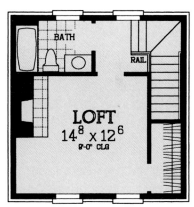

BATH

RAIL

LOFT
14⁸ x 12⁶
9'-0" CLG

PLAN HPT280097

A wide porch graces the entry to this 528-square-foot cottage plan, providing a compact, but fully functional apartment. Mill-turned columns support the roof overhang and the front door opens into the generous living room. A kitchen nook has room for a table and chairs and plenty of overhead cabinets. More storage is available in the bedroom—a large closet with folding doors. A full bath with a tempered glass shower and a linen closet in the hall make this a perfect apartment for an elderly parent or a teen.

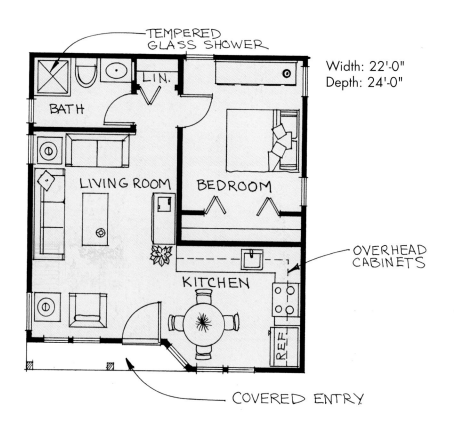

Width: 22'-0"
Depth: 24'-0"

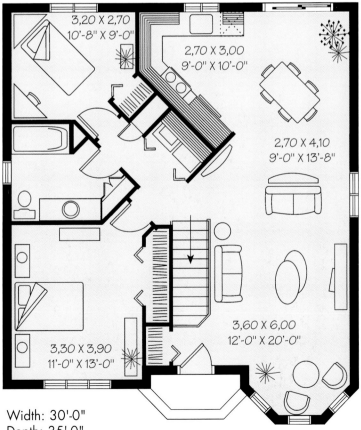

3,20 X 2,70
10'-8" X 9'-0"

2,70 X 3,00
9'-0" X 10'-0"

2,70 X 4,10
9'-0" X 13'-8"

3,30 X 3,90
11'-0" X 13'-0"

3,60 X 6,00
12'-0" X 20'-0"

Width: 30'-0"
Depth: 35'-0"

PLAN HPT280095

An exciting floor plan makes this 972-square-foot home a great starter. The living area is well lighted by windows in the turret and open to the dining area. A sliding door in the dining room leads to the backyard. An angled kitchen counter provides plenty of workspace. A master bedroom shares a full bath with one family bedroom. This home is designed with a basement foundation.

PLAN HPT280099

Lucky are the teenagers who have the option of staking claim to this private retreat! The overall dimensions of 16' x 22' provide 352 square feet of space for study, TV or just hangin' out. Special features include a raised, carpeted platform in the TV lounge; a comfy window seat for reading or a catnap; a separate niche for electronic games; and a unique, brightly painted graffiti wall in the entryway. Wired for sound, bright colors and windows in a variety of shapes mark this specially designed, freestanding building as teens-only territory.

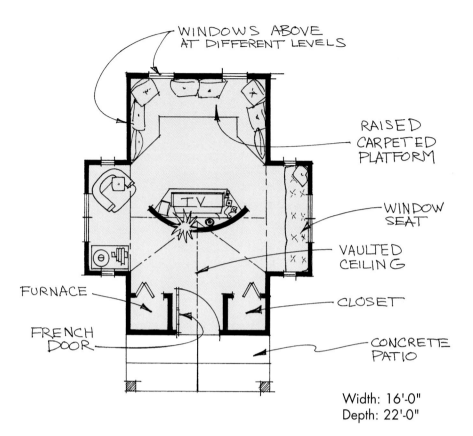

WINDOWS ABOVE AT DIFFERENT LEVELS

RAISED CARPETED PLATFORM

WINDOW SEAT

VAULTED CEILING

CLOSET

CONCRETE PATIO

FURNACE

FRENCH DOOR

TV

Width: 16'-0"
Depth: 22'-0"

PLAN HPT280098

This versatile design features a unique siding pattern: a little bit of country with a pinch of contemporary sophistication. You can build this 320-square-foot, multi-purpose structure on a slab or crawlspace or even with a basement! Planned to take advantage of natural light from all sides, this design will make a perfect studio, game room or office. Or, add a shower in the lavatory room and it becomes a guest house. Features include a half-bath and a kitchen. With all the amenities provided, you could work or relax here for days without ever leaving! The front porch area is a charming place to put your feet up as you or your guests contemplate the events of the day.

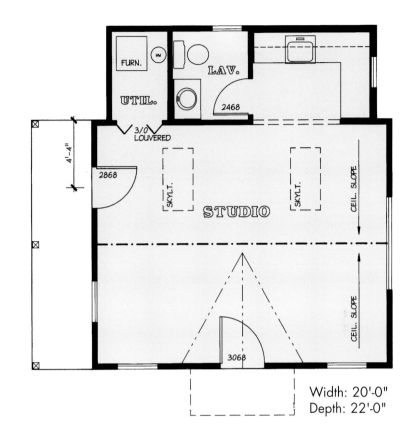

Width: 20'-0"
Depth: 22'-0"

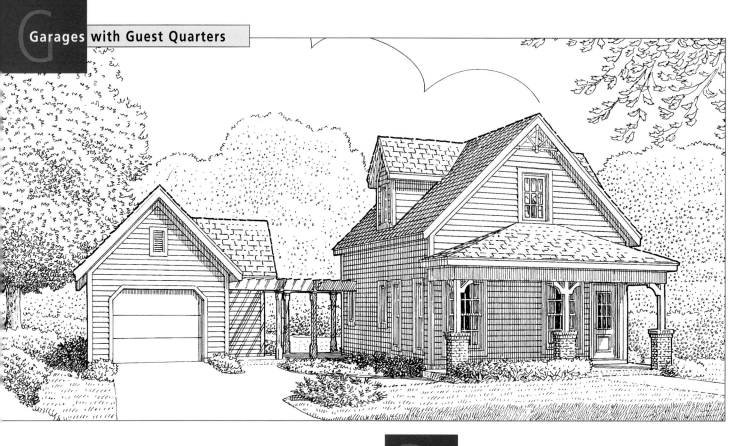

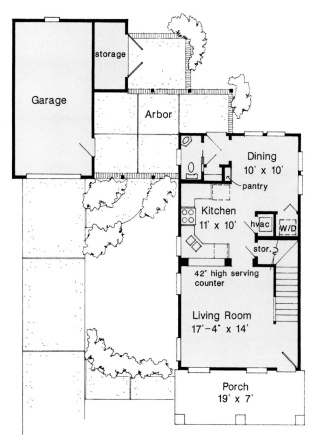

storage

Garage

Arbor

Dining
10' x 10'

pantry

Kitchen
11' x 10'

hvac

W/D

stor.

42" high serving
counter

Living Room
17'-4" x 14'

Porch
19' x 7'

Width: 19'-0"
Depth: 40'-2"

C PLAN HPT280100

This quaint little 985-square-foot Victorian cottage serves perfectly as a starter or second home; or maybe you have it in mind for a lakefront location. Beyond the front porch, the living room defines the front of the house. A full kitchen, a dining room and a powder room account for the back of the house. Each of these areas appreciate an abundance of natural lighting and excellent space utilization. Upstairs, two family bedrooms share a full bath. Bedroom 1 enjoys twin closets. You'll find a detached garage with storage space just beyond the back door and arbor, making a delightful outdoor living space.

Bedroom 1
11'-4" x 11'-8"

5' wall hgt.

8' ceiling

Bath

5' wall hgt.

5'-8" wall hgt.

Bedroom 2
10'-8" x 10'

slope ceiling (typ.)

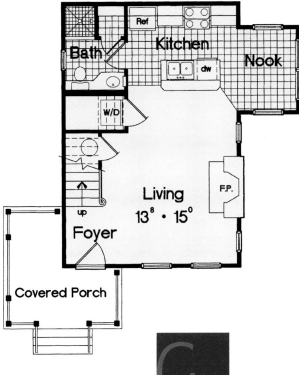

Width: 30'-0"
Depth: 32'-0"

PLAN HPT280101

Designed for one person or a couple, a vacation retreat or a year-round home, this 767-square-foot plan presents simple living with maximum comfort. The corner porch is vast enough for a pair of rocking chairs, and inside, the two-story living room is cozy with a fireplace flanked by windows. The island kitchen boasts a box-bay nook, perfect for every meal of the day. The second floor is dedicated to the master bedroom, which includes a private bath and His and Hers wardrobes.

PLAN HPT280102

Need a quiet place for a home office or studio? You can't go wrong by choosing the plans for this cleverly designed 432-square-foot structure. It is filled with amenities that make a small space seem huge. The ceiling of the main part of the building is vaulted and features clerestory windows to provide ample lighting. Bumped-out areas on both sides are perfect for desks and work areas. A built-in bookshelf along one wall is complemented by a large walk-in storage closet. A half-bath and wet bar round out the plan. The entry is graced by a columned porch and double French doors flanked by fixed windows.

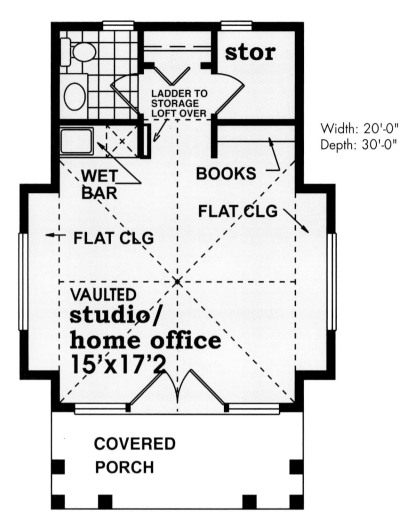

Width: 20'-0"
Depth: 30'-0"

PLAN HPT280103

The ultimate luxury for any craft enthusiast—a separate, free-standing building dedicated to your craft of choice! Functional as well as a beautiful addition to your landscape, this 320-square-foot cottage provides ample counter space and shelving to spread out or store all your materials and tools. And at break time, relax from your hobby in the attached sun room with a vaulted ceiling, French doors and lots of elegant windows. Orient the structure on your property to face south for the sun room and the north-facing work area receives soft, even light. A built-in and well-thought-out work table is flanked by additional countertop work space. Outside, an open 10' x 12' deck off the sun room makes this little cottage just about perfect.

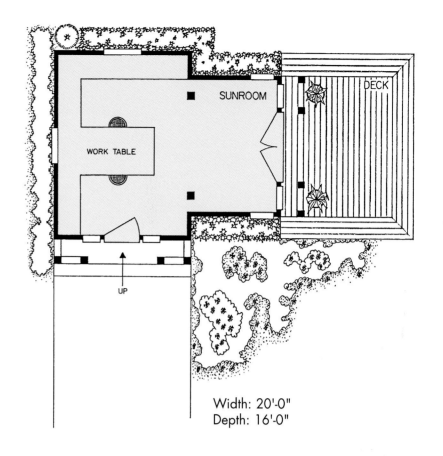

Width: 20'-0"
Depth: 16'-0"

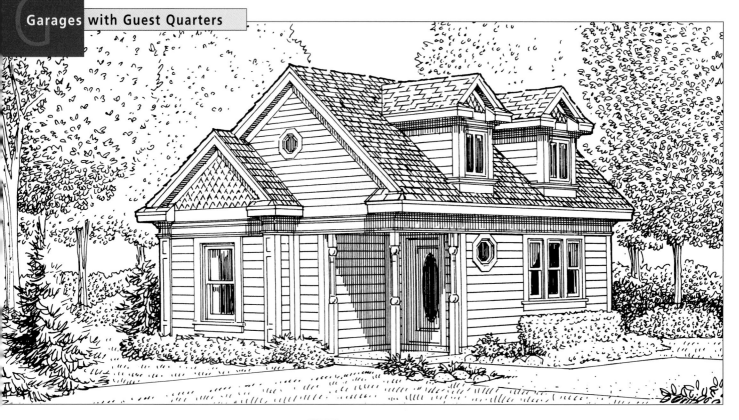

Width: 19'-0"
Depth: 27'-0"

PLAN HPT280104

A lot of living can be packed into this cozy Victorian cottage with a 440-square-foot apartment on the first floor and an additional 126 square feet available in the loft above. The 10' x 10'-8" bedroom and 11' x 15' living room provide plenty of space for one person or a couple. A full bath and kitchenette provide the necessities. A charming dining nook in a sunny bow window and a spiral staircase up to the loft add special touches. It's the perfect answer for keeping watch over aging parents or for use as a home office or weekend guest cottage.

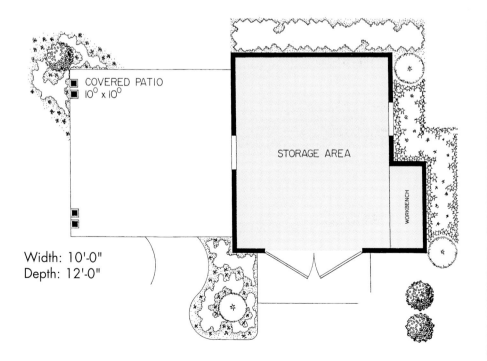

COVERED PATIO
10⁰ x 10⁰

STORAGE AREA

WORKBENCH

Width: 10'-0"
Depth: 12'-0"

PLAN HPT280105

No words quite convey everything this generous storage shed/covered patio combination has to offer. The 120 square feet of storage area presents a delightful facade that belies its practical function. Grooved plywood siding and a shingled double roof are accented by double doors, shutters at the window, a birdhouse tucked in the eaves and a trellis for your favorite climbers. And if that's not enough, the extended roofline covers a 10' x 10' patio area complete with graceful support columns and topped by a jaunty cupola. Use the storage area as a potting shed, storage shed, or workshop.

PLAN HPT280106

This 64-square-foot Victorian playhouse can be the answer to a child's every dream. From the woodcut decorations to the box-bay windows—complete with hidden storage compartments—your children will enjoy hours of playtime in this petite house. Install a child-sized half-door, real windows and paint the exterior in vivid colors and presto! you have a sturdy home that could even be around for your grandchildren. Inside, you can paint the walls with cartoon characters or even paint a faux fireplace on one wall. A vaulted ceiling gives a feeling of space, and the transom windows let sunlight flood in.

Width: 8'-0"
Depth: 8'-0"

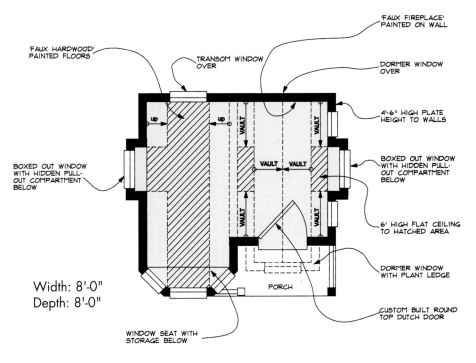

'FAUX HARDWOOD' PAINTED FLOORS

TRANSOM WINDOW OVER

'FAUX FIREPLACE' PAINTED ON WALL

DORMER WINDOW OVER

4'-6" HIGH PLATE HEIGHT TO WALLS

BOXED OUT WINDOW WITH HIDDEN PULL-OUT COMPARTMENT BELOW

BOXED OUT WINDOW WITH HIDDEN PULL-OUT COMPARTMENT BELOW

6' HIGH FLAT CEILING TO HATCHED AREA

DORMER WINDOW WITH PLANT LEDGE

CUSTOM BUILT ROUND TOP DUTCH DOOR

PORCH

WINDOW SEAT WITH STORAGE BELOW

VAULT

PLAN HPT280107

This whimsical, 111-square-foot, scaled-down version of a full-size house makes a dream-come-true playhouse for kids. Featuring a wraparound front porch with a trellis roof, a "real" front door and a loft that can only be reached by a ladder through a trap door! Generous dimensions provide plenty of space for a 7'-4" x 9'-4" play room and a 5'-8" x 6'-4" bunk room. A 7'-4" x 5'-4" loft overlooks the main play area. Natural light floods all areas of this delightful play center through windows in the play room, bunk room, and loft. A sturdy railing borders the loft and the built-in bunk beds in the bunk room are ready and waiting for sleepovers.

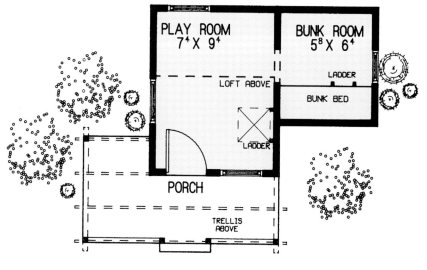

Width: 18'-0"
Depth: 14'-0"

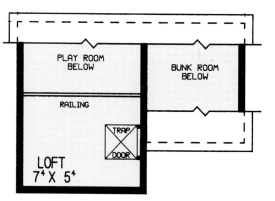

PLAN HPT280108

The kids will love this one! This functional, practical lawn shed doubles in design and capacity as a delightful playhouse complete with a covered porch, lathe-turned columns and a window box for young gardeners. The higher roofline on the shed gives the structure a two-story effect, while the playhouse design gives the simple lawn shed a much more appealing appearance. The 152-square-foot shed is accessed through double doors. The playhouse features a single-door entrance from the porch and three bright windows. The interior wall between the shed and playhouse could be moved another two-and-a-half feet back to make one of the rooms larger. Remove the interior wall completely to use the entire 128-square-foot area exclusively for either the lawn shed or playhouse. The open eaves and porch columns give the structure a country appearance; however, by boxing in the eaves and modifying the columns, you can create just about any style you or the kids like best.

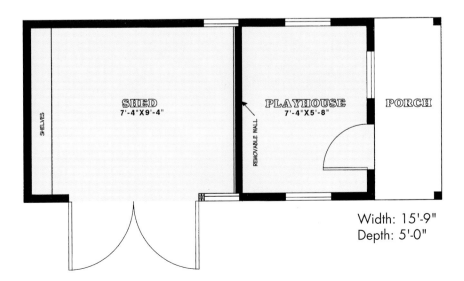

Width: 15'-9"
Depth: 5'-0"

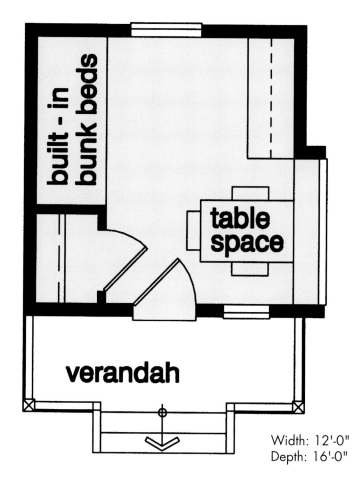

built - in bunk beds

table space

verandah

Width: 12'-0"
Depth: 16'-0"

PLAN HPT280109

For a bare-essentials outdoor structure, this 144-square-foot, weekend cottage offers a wealth of options for its use. Choose it for handy home office space, craft cottage space, extra room for visitors, a playhouse for the kids or a game room. It features a covered front porch and offers two lovely rustic exteriors for you to choose from. The interior has built-in bunk beds, a closet and a bumped-out window that works well for table space. Plans include details for both crawl-space and slab foundations.

PLAN HPT280110

Efficient for Mom and Dad, while munchkin-sized for little people, this 160-square-foot structure boasts practicality and playfulness. The exterior is dazzled in wood siding and cedar shingles—a pleasant display for any outdoor scenery. The garden storage area is separated from the playhouse by a wall and features a sufficient work bench and an illuminating side window. The playhouse resembles a petite version of a country cottage. A tiny covered porch with a wood railing and a window accent the outside and welcome young ones into the petite hideaway. Inside, another window graces the right wall and brightens the interior. There is room enough for a small table and chairs and, most importantly, plenty of toys.

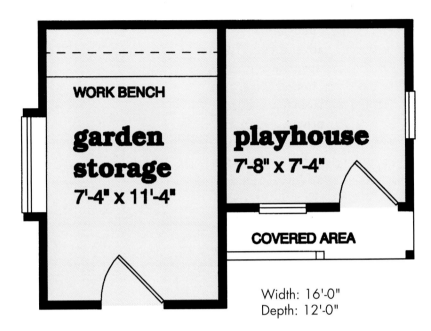

WORK BENCH

garden storage
7'-4" x 11'-4"

playhouse
7'-8" x 7'-4"

COVERED AREA

Width: 16'-0"
Depth: 12'-0"

PLAN HPT280111

This large, 80-square-foot Victorian playhouse is for the kid in all of us. With space enough to hold bunk beds, use it for overnight adventures. Young children will spend hours playing in this little house. Older kids will find it a haven for quiet study or a perfect private retreat. Four windows flood the interior with natural light, and a single-door entrance provides access from the porch. The 8'-1" overall height will accommodate most adults and the addition of electricity and water would expand the versatility of this unit. Designed on a concrete slab, this playhouse could be placed on a wooden frame for future relocation or change in function after the kids leave home.

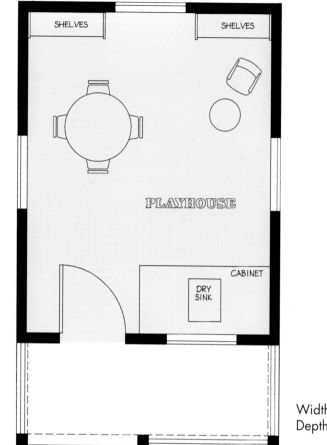

Width: 8'-0"
Depth: 13'-0"

PLAN HPT280112

Lawn shed extraordinaire, this appealing 128-square-foot design can be easily converted from the Tudor style shown here to match just about any exterior design you prefer. In addition to serving as a lawn shed, this versatile structure also can be used as a craft studio, a pool house or a delightful playhouse for your children. The double doors and large floor area provide ample access and storage capacity for lawn tractors and other large pieces of equipment. A handy built-in work bench offers needed space for potting plants or working on craft projects. A separate storage room for craft supplies, lawn-care products or pool chemicals can be locked for safety. Strategically placed on your site, this charming building could be designed to be a reflection of your home in miniature.

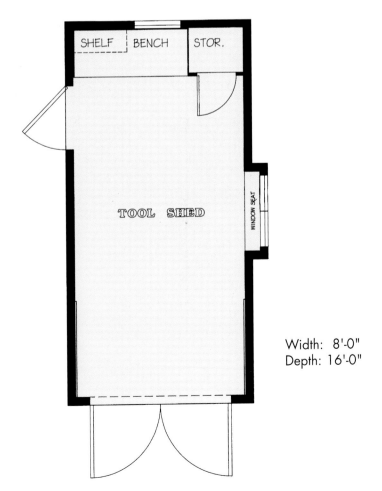

Width: 8'-0"
Depth: 16'-0"

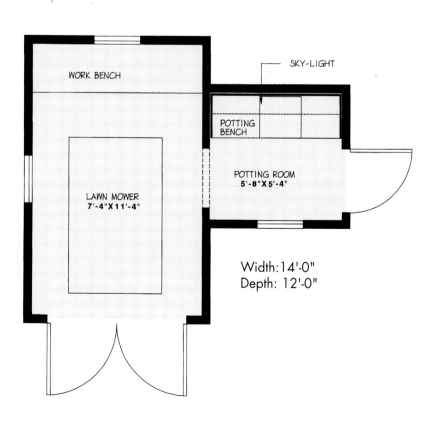

WORK BENCH

SKY-LIGHT

POTTING BENCH

POTTING ROOM
5'-8"X 5'-4"

LAWN MOWER
7'-4"X11'-4"

Width: 14'-0"
Depth: 12'-0"

PLAN HPT280113

Open the double doors of this multi-purpose, 168-square-foot structure and it's a mini-garage for garden tools. Enter by the single door, and it's a potting shed. The tool-shed section is large enough to house the largest lawn tractor, with room to spare for other garden equipment such as shovels, rakes, lawn trimmers and hoses. With windows on all sides and a skylight above the potting bench, the interior has plenty of natural light; the addition of electrical wiring would make this structure even more practical. The design is shown in a Victorian style, but can be modified to match any gable-roof home design.

PLAN HPT280114

This large multi-level garden shed can be easily modified to become a boat house if yours is a nautical family. It encompasses a generous 320 square feet, plus a convenient storage loft, and is totally contemporary in design. As a lawn or garden shed, there is ample room for all your garden equipment, with a separate area for potting plants. The built-in potting bench features removable planks to accommodate flats of flowers in various sizes. The roomy loft provides 133 square feet of safe storage area for chemicals, fertilizers, or other lawn-care products. Natural light floods the interior through multiple windows in the rear wall and in the front, across from the storage loft. This practical structure can also be used as a studio or, placed at the water's edge, it can be easily converted to a boat house by adding 4'x4' columns used as piers in lieu of the slab floor.

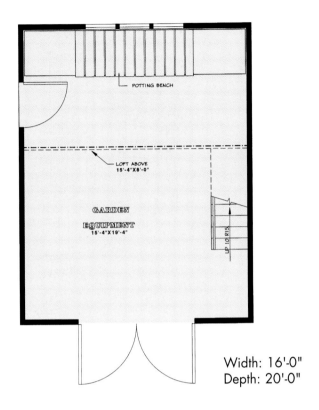

POTTING BENCH

LOFT ABOVE
15'-4"X8'-0"

GARDEN
EQUIPMENT
15'-4"X19'-4"

UP 10 RIS

Width: 16'-0"
Depth: 20'-0"

PLAN HPT280115

Here's a unique design that can be converted to serve a variety of functions: a tool shed, a barbecue stand, a pool-supply depot or a sports-equipment locker. Apply a little "what-if" imagination to come up with additional ways to use this versatile design to enhance your outdoor living space. As a tool shed, this design features a large potting bench with storage above and below. Second, as a summer kitchen, it includes a built-in grill, a sink and a refrigerator. Third, for use as a pool-supply depot or equipment storage, it comes with a locker to store chemicals or valuable sports equipment safely. This structure is designed to be movable but, depending on its function, could be placed on a concrete slab.

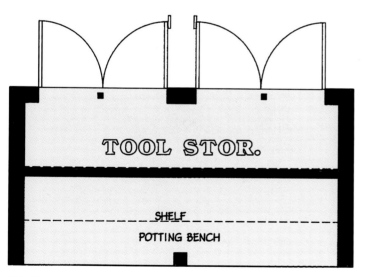

Width: 8'-0"
Depth: 4'-0"

115

PLAN HPT280116

Designed to blend into the garden surroundings, this cozy little building keeps all your garden tools and supplies at your fingertips. You can vary the materials to create the appearance best suited to your site. This 72-square-foot structure is large enough to accommodate a potting bench, shelves, and an area for garden tools. The window above the potting bench allows ample light, but electricity could be added easily. Although the house is designed to be built on a concrete slab, you could use treated lumber for the floor joists, and set it right on the ground. To convert this shed design to a playhouse, simply change the window shelf into a planter and add a step with a handrail at the door.

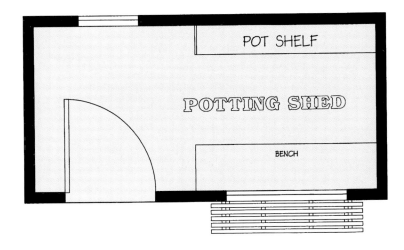

Width: 12'-0"
Depth: 6'-0"

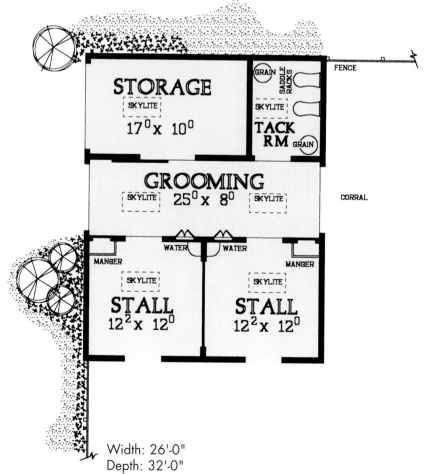

STORAGE
SKYLITE
17⁰ x 10⁰

GRAIN
SADDLE RACKS
SKYLITE
TACK RM
GRAIN

FENCE

GROOMING
SKYLITE 25⁰ x 8⁰ SKYLITE

CORRAL

MANGER
WATER WATER
MANGER
SKYLITE
STALL
12²x 12⁰
SKYLITE
STALL
12²x 12⁰

Width: 26'-0"
Depth: 32'-0"

PLAN HPT280117

With 832 square feet under roof, this expanded structure will be home to your prize stock. Inside, six skylights illuminate the interior of three areas: 1) two 12'-2" x 12' pens with dirt floors, each with built-in feed troughs, fresh-water hookups and Dutch doors leading to an outdoor fenced area; 2) a covered grooming area with sloped, grooved concrete flooring and maximum access through double doors at each end; and 3) a 17' x 10' storage area with concrete floors for hay and a 7'-6" x 10' secured tack room with built-in saddle racks.

PLAN HPT280118

With 832 square feet under roof, this expanded structure will be home to your prize stock. Outside, a 26' x 12' covered area with a concrete floor provides storage and parking for tractors and other equipment. Inside, six skylights illuminate the interior of three major areas: 1) two 12'-2" x 12' stalls with dirt floors, each with built-in feeders, fresh-water hook-ups and Dutch doors leading to an outside pen; 2) a covered grooming area with a slightly sloped, grooved concrete flooring and maximum access though double doors at each end; and 3) a 17' x 10' storage area with concrete floors for feed and a 7'-6" x 10' secured tack room with built-in saddle racks.

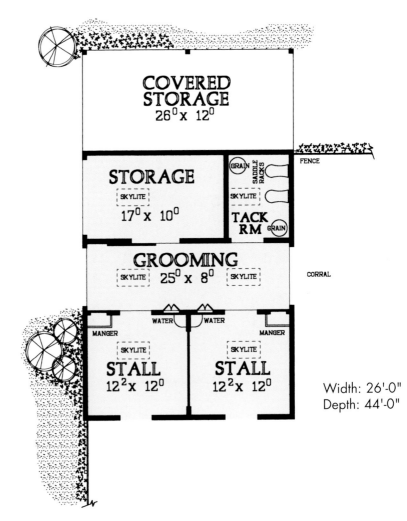

Width: 26'-0"
Depth: 44'-0"

Width: 24'-0"
Depth: 32'-0"

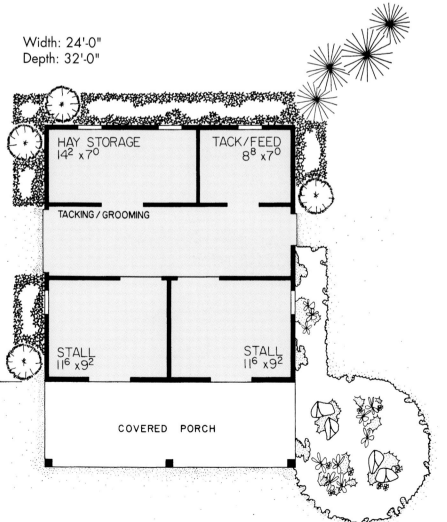

HAY STORAGE
14² x 7⁰

TACK/FEED
8⁸ x 7⁰

TACKING / GROOMING

STALL
11⁶ x 9²

STALL
11⁶ x 9²

COVERED PORCH

PLAN HPT280119

Right out of Kentucky horse country comes this all-in-one design for a two-horse stable, plus tack room and covered hay storage. Two generous 11'-6" x 9'-2" stalls provide shelter and security for your best stock, with easy access through Dutch doors. Against the far wall is a 14'-2" x 7' hay "loft" and next to it, an 8'-8" x 7' tack room. In the center is a large area reserved for grooming your mount or to saddle up for the big race.

G PLAN HPT280120

If you run a large operation, consider this 1,918-square-foot expanded floor plan for your stable requirements. Six 12'-2" x 12' livestock pens with dirt floors feature built-in feed and water troughs and Dutch doors leading either to a fenced exercise area or into either of two conveniently located grooming areas. Both grooming areas have grooved cement floors, sloped for easy hosing and draining. A convenient connecting hall between the grooming areas also has sloped concrete floors for easy maintenance. A central secured tack room with built-in saddle racks and grain bins, a bath with a toilet and sink and a 10' x 17' inside storage area for hay complete the available features. Seven skylights throughout the structure provide an abundance of natural light.

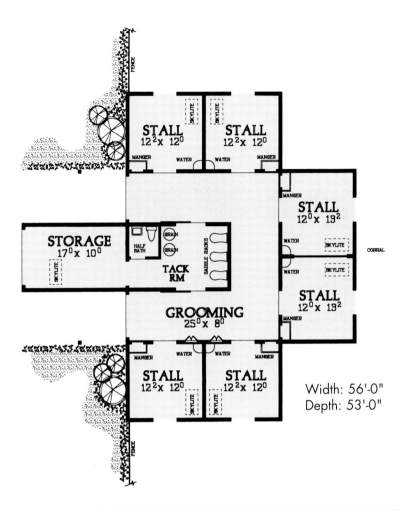

Width: 56'-0"
Depth: 53'-0"

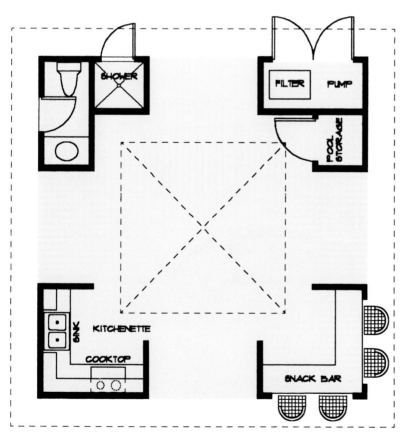

PLAN HPT280121

Entertain the possibilities for poolside parties with this smart, 576-square-foot, multi-functional ramada. Four corner units are united by open-air walkways and are almost literally tied together by a trellis roof. Pull up a chair to the outside bar in one corner for a refreshing drink or snack. Across the walkway is an efficiency kitchenette to make the goodies. In the next corner is a restroom and a shower, each with a separate entrance. The final corner hides all the pool essentials with double doors leading to the filter and pump room and a separate storage room for other pool equipment and toys.

Width: 24'-0"
Depth: 24'-0"

PLAN HPT280122

This 383-square-foot pool pavilion offers a changing room, a summer kitchen and an elegant porch for shade. Add the convenience of bathroom facilities and you're set for outdoor living all summer long. It's designed to provide maximum function in a small area and features built-in benches, shelves, hanging rods and a separate linen closet for towels. The opaque diamond-patterned windows decorate the exterior of the 10'x 6'-8" changing area and the mirror-image bath. The bath could also be made into a kitchen area, then simply add a sliding window to allow easy passage of refreshments to your family and guests at poolside. When you've had enough sun or socializing, recline in the shade under the columned porch and enjoy a good book or a nap.

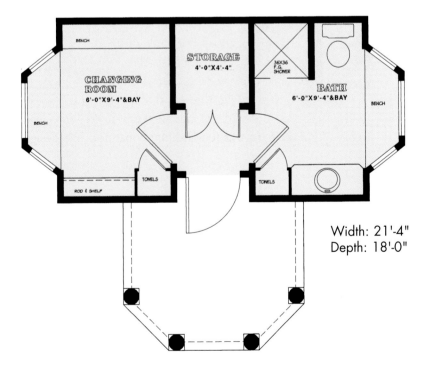

Width: 21'-4"
Depth: 18'-0"

PLAN HPT280123

The magic of this 728-square-foot design is its flexibility. Use it exclusively as a changing cabana with separate His and Hers changing rooms, or, with a little sleight of hand, turn one of the rooms into a summer kitchen for outdoor entertaining. As changing rooms, each eight-sided area includes built-in benches and private bathroom facilities. The kitchen option includes a stove, refrigerator, food-preparation area and a storage pantry. A shuttered window poolside provides easy access to serve your guests across the counter. Linking these two areas is a covered walkway which serves as a shaded picnic area or a convenient place to get out of the sun. Columns, arches and stained-glass windows provide a touch of grandeur to this fun and functional poolside design.

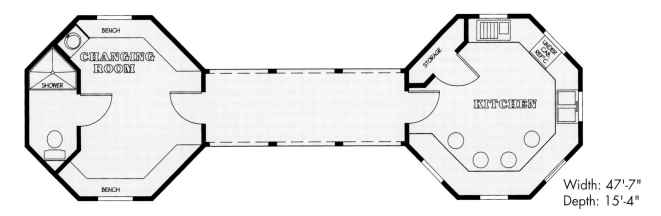

Width: 47'-7"
Depth: 15'-4"

PLAN HPT280124

This 218-square-foot cabana dream complements any poolside manor. A rustic blend of siding and cedar shingles graces the exterior and adds a stylish ornamentation to any private yard. A shaded, quaint covered porch welcomes you to three separate doors. To the right, a private changing chamber offers a bench and linen closet, and is illuminated by a single window. The center room provides a separate outdoor storage area—useful for large or bulky pool equipment such as rafts, games, or tubes. To the left, a private outdoor bathroom is a useful addition. This room is brightened by a window and features a sink, toilet, and separate shower for convenient use. This design can save dozens of trips in and out of the home, providing important efficiency to your private home pool scene.

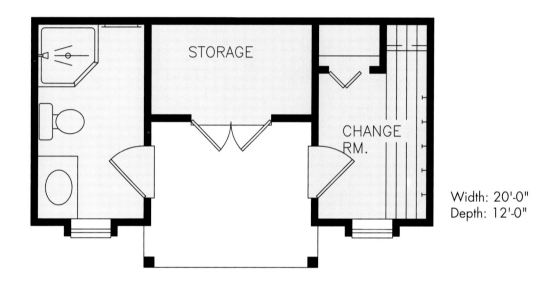

STORAGE

CHANGE RM.

Width: 20'-0"
Depth: 12'-0"

PLAN HPT280125

This 120-square-foot poolside cabana design has a cottage quaintness that will charm any scene. The wood siding and shingle exterior is enhanced by ornamental planter boxes—add bright flowers to decorate your leisurely summer retreat. Two windows naturally brighten the interior. The right side houses a changing room, which features a built-in wood bench and a convenient towel closet. The left room offers an outdoor bathroom, complete with a sink, toilet, and shower area. Practical and comfortable, this cabana easily provides every poolside need.

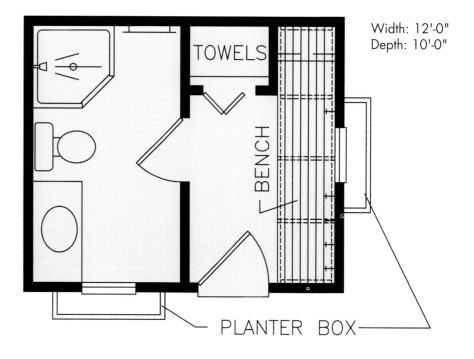

TOWELS

BENCH

Width: 12'-0"
Depth: 10'-0"

PLANTER BOX

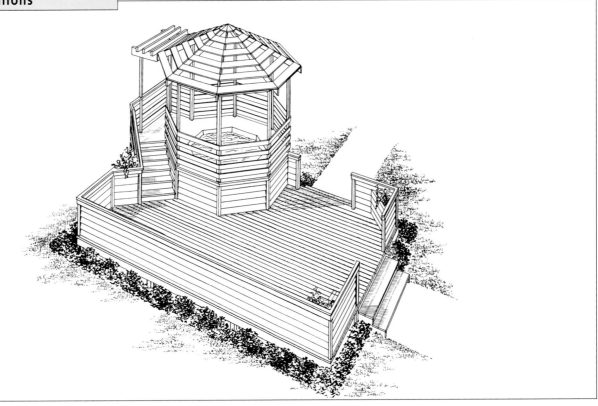

G PLAN HPT280126

Secluded enough for privacy, yet open enough to view the night sky through a curtain of vines on the trellis roof, this private outdoor spa has its own deck with built-in benches and planters. Approximately 280 square feet in area, the deck of this outstanding unit offers plenty of space to entertain friends and family. In the design shown, three steps lead up from the ground to the deck, and six additional steps lead up to the 84" x 84" spa area. Patterned screens and a trellis roof provide privacy. You can place this spa adjacent to your house for convenient access, or install it as a free-standing unit in a secluded area of your property. Easy to build, this design will accommodate a spa of almost any style. The trellis roof can also be modified to a solid roof style or eliminated completely.

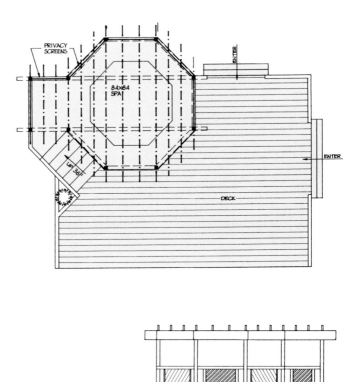

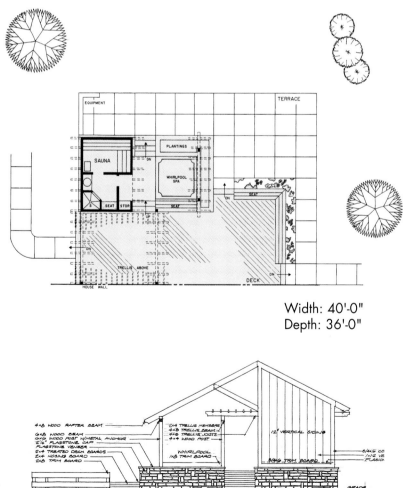

Width: 40'-0"
Depth: 36'-0"

PLAN HPT280127

A relaxing 1,440-square-foot addition to a backyard, this sauna and whirlpool spa combination promises respite from the hectic world. Joined to the house by wood decking and a sun-filtering trellis, the dry-heat sauna has planked seating as well as a sink, shower and a bench seat in the dressing area. A small attached storage room neatly accommodates supplies and equipment. Just outside, raised planters flank the revitalizing whirlpool spa on two sides. The third side has a long bench seat. Additional bench seating borders the wood deck on two sides. Simple lines and an open design allow this plan to blend perfectly with any style or type of house.

127

PLAN HPT280128

An outdoor kitchen and much, much more! For year-round, daylight-to-dark entertaining, consider this large outdoor entertainment unit. Nearly 700 square feet of floor space includes a deck for sunbathing by day or dancing under the stars after sundown. A 13' x 13'-2" screened room provides a pest-free environment for cards or conversation. And, the cookout chef will rule with a flair over a full-service kitchen area that may include a grill, wet bar, sink, refrigerator and ample room for storage. You can locate this versatile structure adjacent to your pool, or place it as a free-standing unit wherever your landscape and site plan allow. Select material for the railings and privacy screens in patterns to match or complement your home.

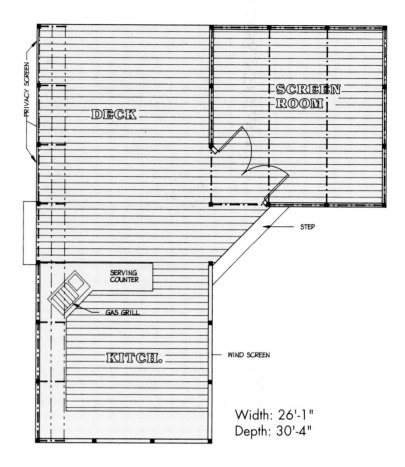

PRIVACY SCREEN

DECK

SCREEN ROOM

STEP

SERVING COUNTER

GAS GRILL

KITCH.

WIND SCREEN

Width: 26'-1"
Depth: 30'-4"

PLAN HPT280129

In the days before modern fire protection, kitchens were established as separate buildings away from the main house for safety reasons. No longer a necessity, a separate summer kitchen is a charming option for cooking outdoors. In this over 600-square-foot design, a spacious deck connects the barbecue area with its generous counter space and storage, with the covered cooking area complete with sink, stove and refrigerator. Translucent panels in the roof provide lots of natural light. There is ample room under the roof for a table and chairs and you can enclose this area with screen panels to keep out flying insects. Built-in benches adjacent to the barbecue provide additional seating or serving space.

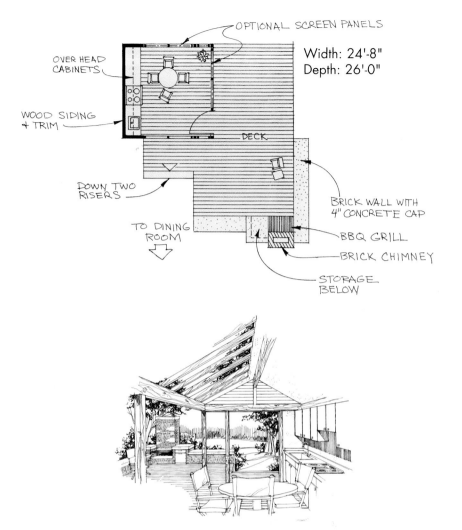

OPTIONAL SCREEN PANELS

OVER HEAD CABINETS

WOOD SIDING + TRIM

Width: 24'-8"
Depth: 26'-0"

DECK

DOWN TWO RISERS

TO DINING ROOM

BRICK WALL WITH 4" CONCRETE CAP

BBQ GRILL

BRICK CHIMNEY

STORAGE BELOW

PLAN HPT280130

This petite 64-square-foot pavilion design is perfect for private and refreshing entertaining. Build this structure close to a pool area to save trips in and out of the home kitchen. Summer leisure time can be more comfortably spent with this convenience close at hand. A refrigerator space is generously provided alongside a counter preparation area. Above, built-in shelves may be added for extra storage. On the opposite side, a bar counter resides for accessible convenience.

REF. SPACE

BAR COUNTER

Width: 8'-0"
Depth: 8'-0"

PLAN HPT280131

This stylish 128-square-foot pavilion is an amusing outdoor retreat for any family. A hipped roof shades the inner area—keep a picnic table close by for outdoor barbecues and entertaining. To the right, a barbecue area is provided for outdoor grilling next to a convenient work counter—useful for preparing outdoor meals. A refrigerator space is also provided, next to another counter, for keeping cool foods fresh. The pavilion is completed by a bar counter, large enough to host a wide variety of refreshments. Decorate the outer perimeters with garden side plants. Built for the family that excels in entertaining, this structure is a lively addition to any property.

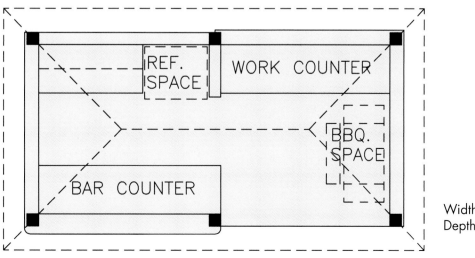

Width: 16'-0"
Depth: 8'-0"

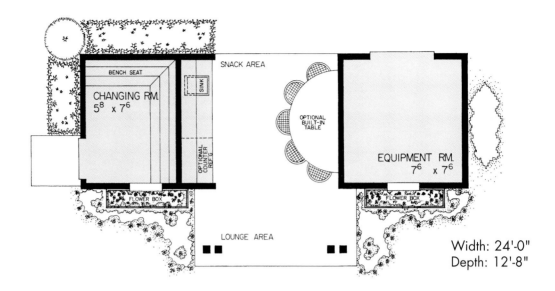

BENCH SEAT

CHANGING RM.
5⁸ x 7⁶

SINK

SNACK AREA

OPTIONAL
BUILT-IN
TABLE

OPTIONAL COUNTER REF'G

EQUIPMENT RM.
7⁶ x 7⁶

FLOWER BOX

FLOWER BOX

LOUNGE AREA

Width: 24'-0"
Depth: 12'-8"

PLAN HPT280132

You can enhance both the beauty and the function of any pool area with this charming structure. A mini-kitchen and an optional built-in table are tucked in the breezeway of this double-room; you'll have shelter for poolside repasts no matter what the weather. The exterior features include a gable roof with columns in the front, shuttered windows, horizontal wood and shingle siding, decorative flower boxes, and a cupola. The two rooms on either side of the breezeway area provide a 5'-8"x7'-6" changing area with built-in seating and a larger area—7'-6"x7'-6"—for convenient storage for pool supplies and equipment. This spacious cabana is sure to be a fine addition to an active family's pool area.

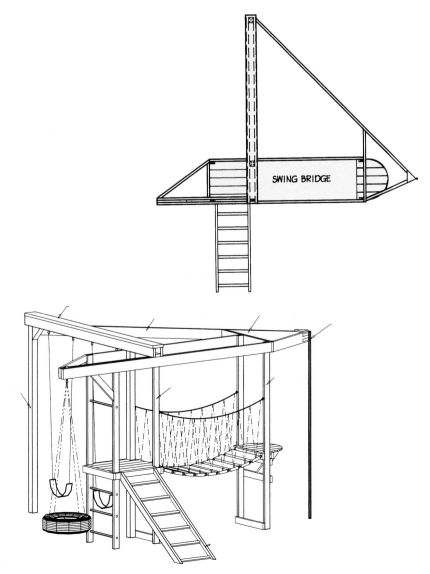

SWING BRIDGE

PLAN HPT280133

The highlight of this delightful playset is the swinging bridge. It is available ready-made in a variety of styles or you can make it yourself. Either way, be sure to check that the handrail is high enough to prevent small children from toppling over the top or falling through the sides. Designed for kids five and older, this playset includes a ladder inset at an angle to help developmental coordination. Both shelf-style swings and a popular tire swing are provided for variety. Hardware for the swings is available from your local suppliers. For larger tire swings, simply extend the support beam to accept a larger swing area. This playset is designed to sit on the ground; however, the firefighter's pole should be sunk into the ground six to eight inches to give it additional stability.

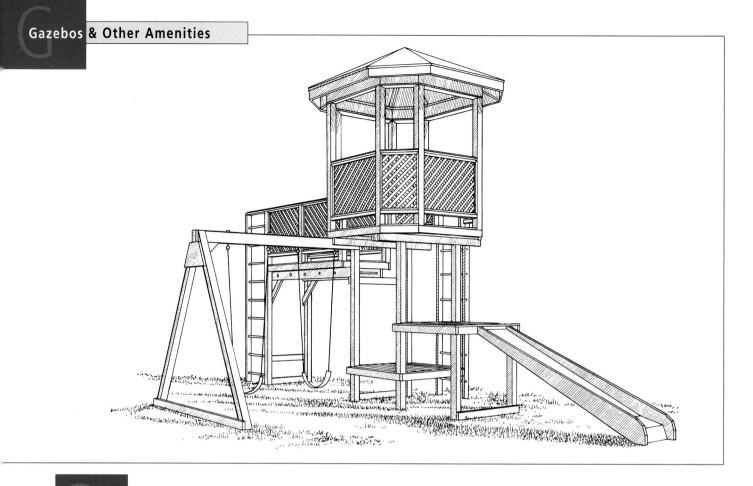

G PLAN HPT280134

A playhouse, a tree house, a lookout tower...your children will invent many uses for this mini-gazebo perched almost eight feet above the ground. It's large enough for a small table and chairs for a picnic or a Mad Hatter's tea party. Or, spread out some sleeping bags and invite friends for an overnight adventure—but no sleepwalking! The ladder, swings and slide all add to the fun and can be modified to accommodate the ages of your children. If you have a full-size gazebo on your site, or plan to build one, you could use a similar design in the railings for both units for a surprising "double-take" effect.

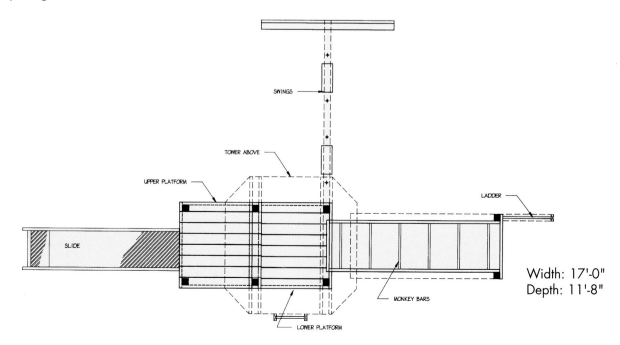

SWINGS

TOWER ABOVE

UPPER PLATFORM

LADDER

SLIDE

MONKEY BARS

LOWER PLATFORM

Width: 17'-0"
Depth: 11'-8"

PLAN HPT280135

A playset with a little bit of every-thing. This playset is designed to use any of the shelf-style swing units available at your local supplier. There are two slides—one regular, the other an enclosed spiral slide to provide added thrills. The ramp is designed for kids who like to climb back up the slide. Now they can climb up the ramp and slide down the other side. For small children, you can add a knotted rope to help them up. The climb to the Eagle's Nest will provide your kids with exercise for their muscles and their imagination. Young children will love to switch from one part of this play-set to another, over and over again.

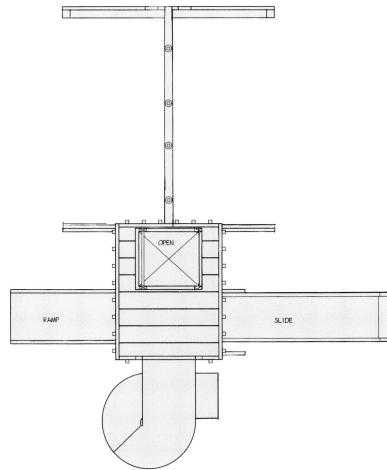

RAMP

OPEN

SLIDE

PLAN HPT280136

When it comes to playhouses, it just doesn't get much better than this. Any child's imagination will sail over mysterious, unknown seas every time he or she enters this playhouse. No matter what flag is flown—that of Captain Hook, Davey Jones, or Queen Isabella—this playhouse will offer kids years of enjoyment. More than 15 feet from stem to stern, this unique playhouse is easier to build than it looks. Constructed entirely of standard materials, the design includes a cannon on the main deck and gun ports in the hold that pull open to simulate a real Spanish galleon. A concrete foundation is recommended for this structure, due to its overall height—9'-5½"—and the number of children who will be sailing off to wonderful places.

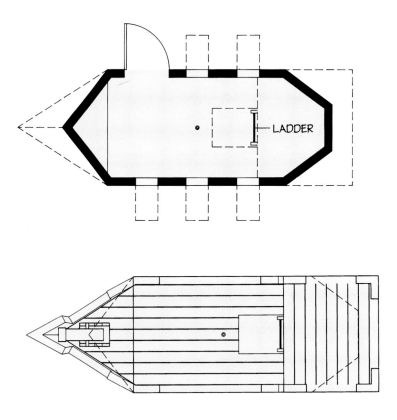

PLAN HPT280137

Lords and ladies, knights and evil-doers—this playhouse has everything except a fire-breathing dragon! Your children will spend hours re-enacting the days of Kings and Queens and Knights of the Round Table. Surprisingly easy to build, this playset right out of King Arthur's Court uses standard materials. One corner of the playhouse holds a 4' x 4' sandbox. A stairway leads to a 3' x 3' tower with its own catwalk. The area under the stairway could be enclosed to make a storage room for toys...or a dungeon to hold the captured Black Knight. The double castle doors can be fitted with standard hardware, but wrought-iron hinges will make this innovative playhouse look even more like a castle.

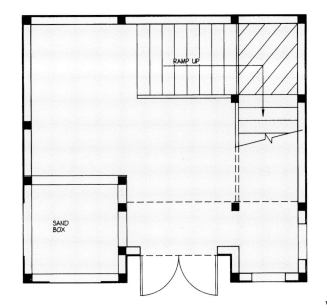

Width: 11'-0"
Depth: 10'-0"

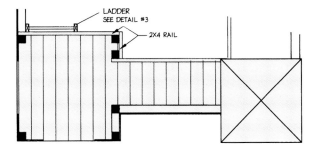

137

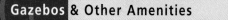

G PLAN HPT280138

Nostalgia unlimited—this romantic covered bridge will re-create a unique link to history on your site. It is patterned after functional bridges built in the 1700s and 1800s, which were intended to provide a dry resting place for weary travelers. This current-day design offers expandable dimensions for a 12', 14' or 16' span. To cross a wider area, the span can be increased by multiples of those dimensions, using larger floor joists. Check with your local supplier for the span capability of the joists you employ in your project. The sides of this "glimpse into the past" have open window areas to allow air to flow freely. The generous 5'-3½" width allows for safe passage of any standard garden tractor or mower.

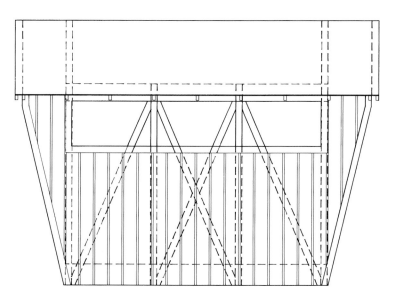

PLAN HPT280139

Combine form, function and beauty in this appealing bridge to enhance your landscape and provide easy passage over wet or rocky terrain. Entrance and exit ramps at either end of the bridge replicate the gentle arch of the handrail. The plans for this functional addition show how to build 6', 8' or 10' spans to meet your needs. The decorative railing pattern will add a touch of elegance and charm to any site.

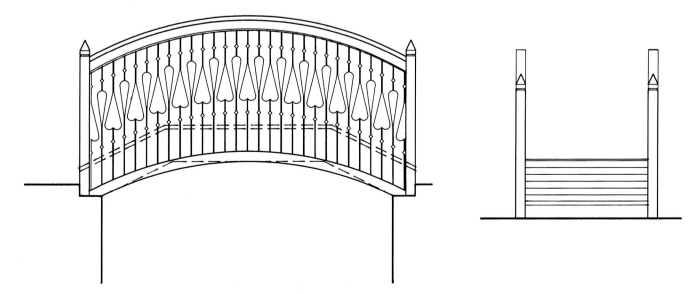

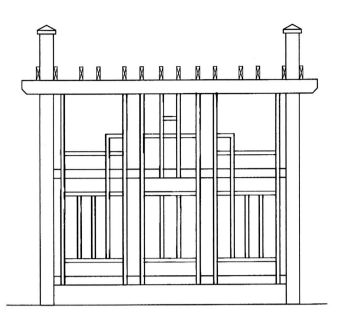

PLAN HPT280140

Build this impressive arbor to cover a garden path or walkway. Add the matching bench inside the arbor as a plant shelf or to provide shaded seating. Use the bench outside as an accent to both the arbor and the surrounding landscape. The 7'-11" patterned back and 5'-11" x 8'-1½" trellis roof are ideal for climbing vines or roses, giving this beautiful arbor even more of a garden effect. The 8'-11" bench is wide enough to seat four or five adults comfortably. The latticework design is repeated on the back and sides of the bench. The arbor is designed to sit on a slab, or you can sink the support columns right into the ground using pressure-treated materials.

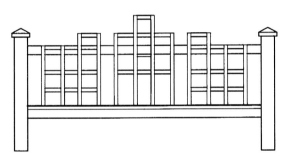

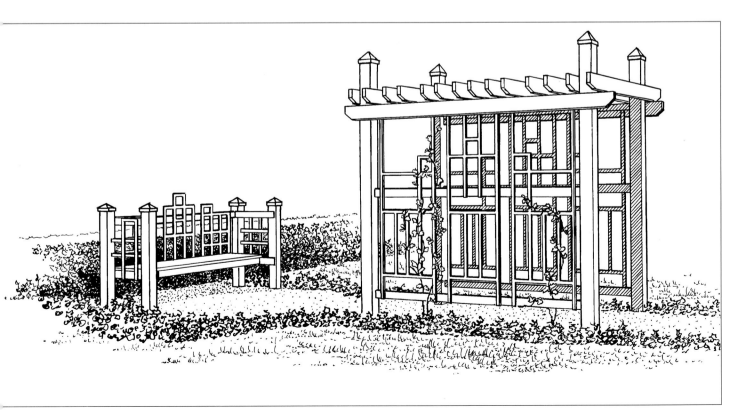

C PLAN HPT280141

You can create a cozy shaded nook for reading or relaxing with this appealing strombrella. It's simple to build as a glider or with a fixed seat. Either option provides ample room for two or three people to sit comfortably. Both designs use standard materials. For a fixed unit, attach it to a cement slab. To make it moveable, use a wood base. Cover the roof with basic asphalt or fiberglass shingles, or use cedar shake shingles to enhance the appearance.

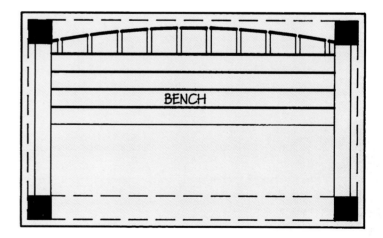

BENCH

Width: 6'-0"
Depth: 3'-6"

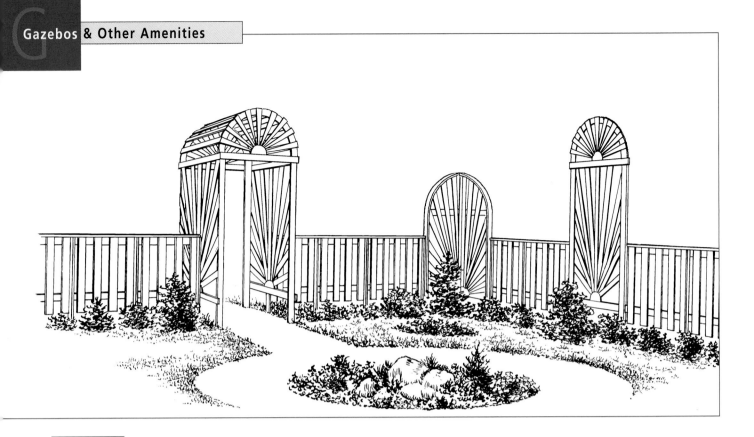

G PLAN HPT280142

A distinctive sunburst pattern is repeated in each element of this attractive and versatile 8' garden arbor. Train your favorite vines over the slat roof to provide shade for the flower beds below or for the roses climbing along the 1'x6' slat-fence extensions. Also included in this package are plans for a 4' corner trellis which can be used to extend the sunburst pattern to other areas of your landscape and serve as an accent in flower beds or planters. This arbor—with its sunburst effect—offers a warm and welcoming focal point to any yard or garden area.

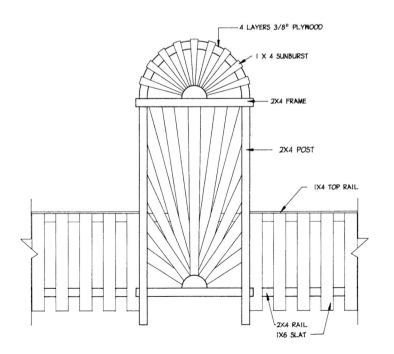

4 LAYERS 3/8" PLYWOOD

1 X 4 SUNBURST

2X4 FRAME

2X4 POST

1X4 TOP RAIL

2X4 RAIL
1X6 SLAT

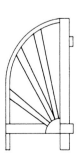

PLAN HPT280143

An accent to gracious living, this classic strombrella will create an elegant focal point in any garden or landscape. Evoking memories of a more slowly paced era, the design is similar to those built in the late 1800s. The bench is large enough to seat up to six people. To increase its function, a half-round pole table could be added to provide a small picnic area or a nook for reading, cards or quiet conversation. The millwork can be purchased from your local supplier or from the manufacturer listed on the construction drawings. The generous entrance is four feet wide and could provide space for additional seating if needed. You can build this structure with a wood base to allow for movable feasts, or secure it to a slab to make it permanent.

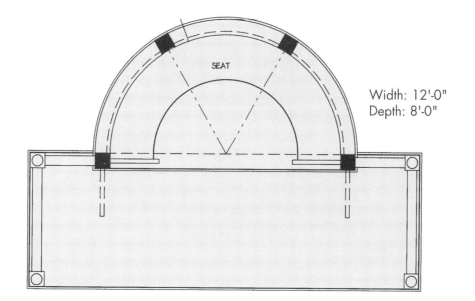

SEAT

Width: 12'-0"
Depth: 8'-0"

PLAN HPT282001

Shining copper on the cupola and shimmering glass windows all around enhance this double-entrance gazebo with dancing light and color. The many windows allow natural light to engulf the interior, making it a perfect studio. Easy to heat and cool, this gazebo contains operable louvers in the cupola to increase the flow of air. An exhaust fan could be added to the cupola to further maximize air flow. The masonry base with brick steps gives the structure a definite feeling of both elegance and permanence.

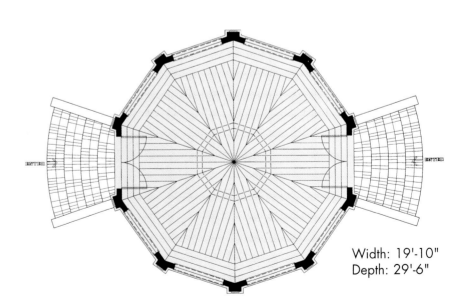

Width: 19'-10"
Depth: 29'-6"

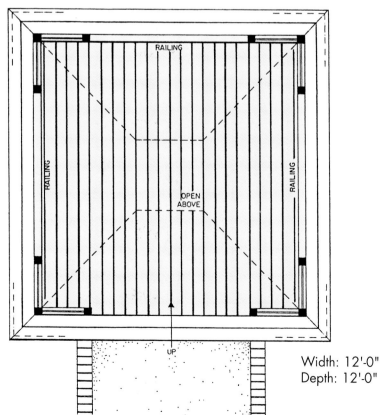

Width: 12'-0"
Depth: 12'-0"

PLAN HPT282002

Best suited for larger lots, this gazebo provides a prime spot for entertaining. With 144 square feet, it has as much surface space as the average family room. And, topping out at just under 17½ feet, it's as tall as a one-story house! Boasting many neoclassic features—perfect proportions, columns and bases—it blends well with a variety of housing styles: Cape Cod, Georgian, farmhouse and others. The cupola is an added touch that allows for ventilation. Cedar or redwood would be a good choice for building materials.

PLAN HPT282003

Designed for serious entertaining, the size alone—162 square feet—ensures you that this gazebo is unique. The star-lattice railing design, built-in benches and raised center roof with accent trim make this structure as practical as it is attractive. Large enough for small parties, there is built-in seating for about twenty people and enough floor area for another ten to twenty. Ideal for entertaining, the addition of lights and a wet bar make this design an important extension of any home.

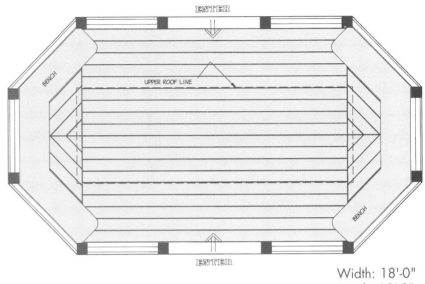

Width: 18'-0"
Depth: 10'-0"

PLAN HPT282004

Victorian on a small scale, this gazebo will be the highlight of any yard. With a cupola topped by a weathervane, a railed perimeter and double steps up, it's the essence of historic design. Small enough to fit on just about any size lot, yet large enough to accommodate a small crowd, it is perfect for outdoor entertaining with 114 square feet of space. Choose standard gingerbread details from your local supplier to make it your own.

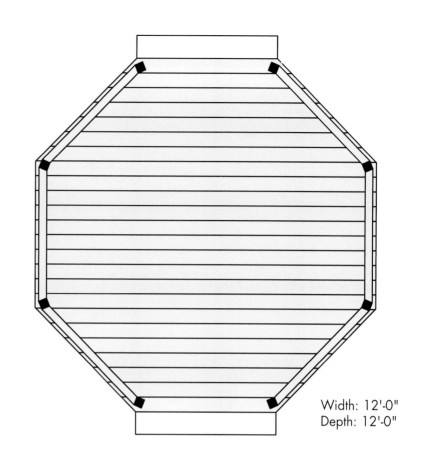

Width: 12'-0"
Depth: 12'-0"

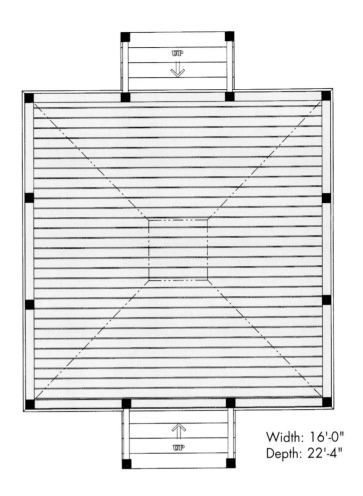

PLAN HPT280148

Dance the night away in this double-entrance, pass-through style gazebo. By day, the open-air construction provides a clear view in all directions. The large floor area of 256 square feet seats 12 to 16 people comfortably or nicely accommodates musicians or entertainers for a lawn party. The decorative cupola can be lowered, louvered, or removed to create just the appearance you want. Or, add an antique weathervane just for fun. This gazebo has five steps up, which give it a large crawlspace for access to any added utilities. Its square shape allows for simple cutting and floor framing, plus easy assembly of the roof frame. The trim and hand rails are simple to construct or modify to achieve several different design effects.

Width: 16'-0"
Depth: 22'-4"

PLAN HPT280149

Reflecting the image "gingerbread" is intended to convey, this delightful gazebo will be the focal point of your landscape . . . the icing on the cake . . . the star atop the holiday tree! The floor area of nearly 144 square feet is large enough for a table and chairs. Or, add built-in benches to increase the seating capacity to accommodate twenty people. Painted white with pink asphalt roof shingles, this gazebo has a cool, summery appearance. Or, you can build it with unpainted, treated materials and cedar shake shingles for an entirely different effect. Either exterior design will provide an outstanding setting for years of outdoor relaxation and entertainment. The jaunty cupola complete with spire adds a stately look to this single-entrance structure. The plans also include an optional arbor, which can be incorporated into the entrance of the gazebo.

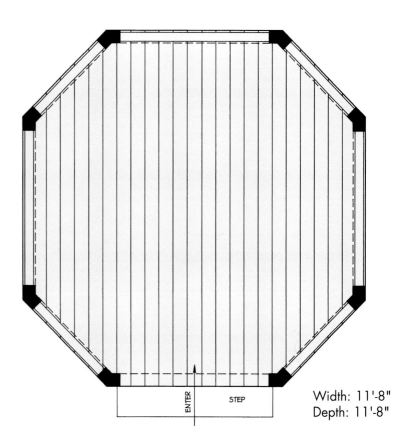

ENTER   STEP

Width: 11'-8"
Depth: 11'-8"

PLAN HPT280150

This all-American single-entrance gazebo is simple to construct and easy to adapt to a variety of styles. All materials are available in most areas with no special cutting for trim or rails. This gazebo is distinguished by its simple design and large floor area. The traditional eight-sided configuration and overall area of approximately 160 square feet allow for the placement of furniture with ample seating for 8 to 10 people. Build as shown, or modify the trim and railings to give a totally different appearance. If multiple entrance/exit access is desired, simply eliminate the rails as needed. Access to the ground is a single step, which could be easily modified for a low ramp.

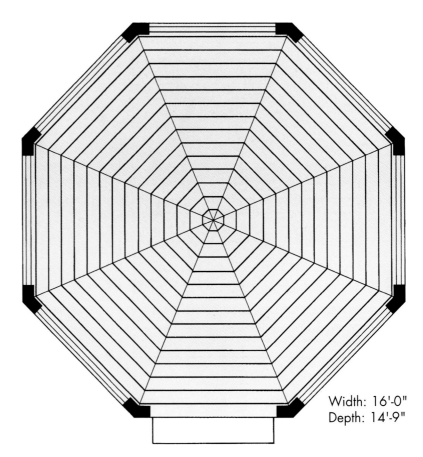

Width: 16'-0"
Depth: 14'-9"

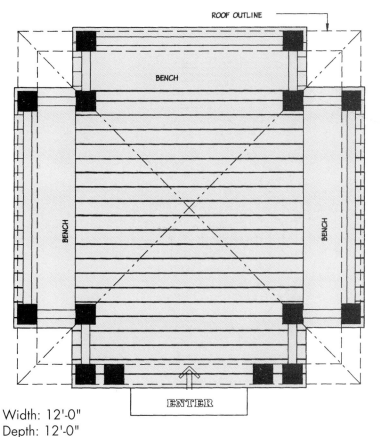

ROOF OUTLINE

BENCH

BENCH

BENCH

ENTER

Width: 12'-0"
Depth: 12'-0"

PLAN HPT280151

Up, down, and green all around! Light and airy, the unique trellis roof of this innovative single-entrance gazebo is just waiting for your favorite perennial vines. To extend the green-all-around look, modify the railings to a lattice pattern and train vines or grapes—or roses, for a splash of color—to experience nature all around you. The inset corners of the design provide plenty of space for planting. Simple lines make this delightful gazebo easy to construct, with no cumbersome cutting or gingerbread. The large area—128 square feet—provides built-in seating for 9 people. This flexible design could be modified to a closed roof with any standard roof sheathing and shingles, and the single-entrance design can be altered to accommodate multiple entrances.

PLAN HPT280152

The built-in planters and open roof areas of this multiple-entrance gazebo make this design a gardener's dream-come-true. The open roof allows sun and rain ample access to the planters and gives the structure a definite country-garden effect. Built with or without a cupola, the open lattice work in the walls and roof will complement a wide variety of landscapes and home designs. A creative gardener will soon enhance this charming gazebo with a wealth of plants and vines. Tuck a bird bath or bubbling fountain into a corner to further the garden setting. The large design—256 square feet—ensures that both you and nature have plenty of room to share all this gazebo has to offer. It easily accommodates a table and chairs when you invite your guests to this outdoor hideaway.

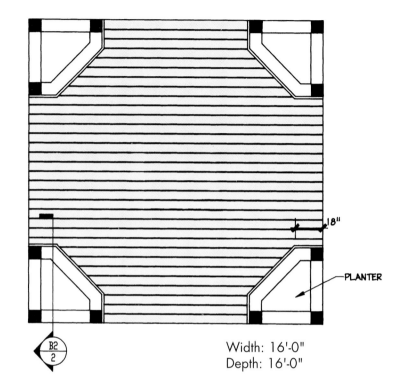

Width: 16'-0"
Depth: 16'-0"

LET US SHOW YOU OUR HOME BLUEPRINT PACKAGE.

BUILDING A HOME? PLANNING A HOME?

OUR BLUEPRINT PACKAGE HAS NEARLY EVERYTHING YOU NEED TO GET THE JOB DONE RIGHT,

whether you're working on your own or with help from an architect, designer, builder or subcontractors. Each Blueprint Package is the result of many hours of work by licensed architects or professional designers.

QUALITY

Hundreds of hours of painstaking effort have gone into the development of your blueprint plan. Each home has been quality-checked by professionals to insure accuracy and buildability.

VALUE

Because we sell in volume, you can buy professional quality blueprints at a fraction of their development cost. With our plans, your dream home design costs substantially less than the fees charged by architects.

SERVICE

Once you've chosen your favorite home plan, you'll receive fast, efficient service whether you choose to mail or fax your order to us or call us toll free at 1-800-521-6797. After you have received your order, call for customer service toll free 1-888-690-1116.

SATISFACTION

Over 50 years of service to satisfied home plan buyers provide us unparalleled experience and knowledge in producing quality blueprints.

ORDER TOLL FREE 1-800-521-6797

After you've looked over our Blueprint Package and Important Extras, call toll free on our Blueprint Hotline: 1-800-521-6797, for current pricing and availability prior to mailing the order form on page 157. We're ready and eager to serve you. After you have received your order, call for customer service toll free 1-888-690-1116.

Each set of blueprints is an interrelated collection of detail sheets which includes components such as floor plans, interior and exterior elevations, dimensions, cross-sections, diagrams and notations. These sheets show exactly how your house is to be built.

SETS MAY INCLUDE:

FRONTAL SHEET
This artist's sketch of the exterior of the house gives you an idea of how the house will look when built and landscaped. Large floor plans show all levels of the house and provide an overview of your new home's livability, as well as a handy reference for deciding on furniture placement.

FOUNDATION PLANS
This sheet shows the foundation layout including support walls, excavated and unexcavated areas, if any, and foundation notes. If slab construction rather than basement, the plan shows footings and details for a monolithic slab. This page, or another in the set, may include a sample plot plan for locating your house on a building site.

DETAILED FLOOR PLANS
These plans show the layout of each floor of the house. Rooms and interior spaces are carefully dimensioned and keys are given for cross-section details provided later in the plans. The positions of electrical outlets and switches are shown.

HOUSE CROSS-SECTIONS
Large-scale views show sections or cut-aways of the foundation, interior walls, exterior walls, floors, stairways and roof details. Additional cross-sections may show important changes in floor, ceiling or roof heights or the relationship of one level to another. Extremely valuable for construction, these sections show exactly how the various parts of the house fit together.

INTERIOR ELEVATIONS
Many of our drawings show the design and placement of kitchen and bathroom cabinets, laundry areas, fireplaces, bookcases and other built-ins. Little "extras," such as mantelpiece and wainscoting drawings, plus molding sections, provide details that give your home that custom touch.

EXTERIOR ELEVATIONS
These drawings show the front, rear and sides of your house and give necessary notes on exterior materials and finishes. Particular attention is given to cornice detail, brick and stone accents or other finish items that make your home unique.

BLUEPRINT PRICE SCHEDULE

Prices guaranteed through December 31, 2002

TIERS	1-SET STUDY PACKAGE	4-SET BUILDING PACKAGE	8-SET BUILDING PACKAGE	1-SET REPRODUCIBLE*
P1	$20	$50	$90	$140
P2	$40	$70	$110	$160
P3	$70	$100	$140	$190
P4	$100	$130	$170	$220
P5	$140	$170	$210	$270
P6	$180	$210	$250	$310
A1	$440	$480	$520	$660

* Requires a fax number

OPTIONS FOR PLANS IN TIER A1

Additional Identical Blueprints
in same order for "A1–L4" price plans ....$50 per set
Reverse Blueprints (mirror image)
with 4- or 8-set order for "A1–L4" plans..$50 fee per order
Specification Outlines...$10 each

IMPORTANT NOTES

• The 1-set study package is marked "not for construction."
• Prices for 4- or 8-set Building Packages honored only at time of original order.
• Some foundations carry a $225 surcharge.
• Right-reading reverse blueprints, if available, will incur a $165 surcharge.
• Additional identical blueprints may be purchased within 60 days of original order.

TO USE THE INDEX,

refer to the design number listed in numerical order (a helpful page reference is also given). Note the price tier and refer to the Blueprint Price Schedule above for the cost of one, four or eight sets of blueprints or the cost of a reproducible drawing. Additional prices are shown for identical and reverse blueprint sets.

TO ORDER,

Call toll free 1-800-521-6797 for current pricing and availability prior to mailing the order form. FAX: 1-800-224-6699 or 520-544-3086.

SPECIFICATION OUTLINE

This valuable 16-page document is critical to building your house correctly. Designed to be filled in by you or your builder, this book lists 166 stages or items crucial to the building process. It provides a comprehensive review of the construction process and helps in choosing materials. When combined with the blueprints, a signed contract, and a schedule, it becomes a legal document and record for the building of your home.

OPTIONS FOR PLANS IN TIERS P1–P6

Additional Identical Blueprints
in same order for "P1–P6" price plans..$10 per set
Reverse Blueprints (mirror image) for "P1–P6" price plans ....$10 fee per order
1 Set of Gazebo Construction Details ....$14.95 each
Gazebo Construction Package ....**add $10 to Building Package price**
(includes 1 set of "P1–P6" plans, plus
1 set Standard Gazebo Construction Details)

BEFORE FILLING OUT

THE ORDER FORM,

PLEASE CALL US ON

OUR TOLL-FREE

BLUEPRINT HOTLINE

1-800-521-6797.

YOU MAY WANT TO

LEARN MORE ABOUT

OUR SERVICES AND

PRODUCTS. HERE'S

SOME INFORMATION

YOU WILL FIND HELPFUL.

OUR EXCHANGE POLICY

With the exception of reproducible plan orders, we will exchange your entire first order for an equal or greater number of blueprints within our plan collection within 90 days of the original order. The entire content of your original order must be returned before an exchange will be processed. Please call our customer service department for your return authorization number and shipping instructions. If the returned blueprints look used, redlined or copied, we will not honor your exchange. Fees for exchanging your blueprints are as follows: 20% of the amount of the original order...plus the difference in cost if exchanging for a design in a higher price bracket or less the difference in cost if exchanging for a design in a lower price bracket. **(Reproducible blueprints are not exchangeable or refundable.)** Please call for current postage and handling prices. Shipping and handling charges are not refundable.

ABOUT REPRODUCIBLES

When purchasing a reproducible you may be required to furnish a fax number. The designer will fax documents that you must sign and return to them before shipping will take place.

ABOUT REVERSE BLUEPRINTS

Although lettering and dimensions will appear backward, reverses will be a useful aid if you decide to flop the plan. See Price Schedule and Plans Index for pricing.

REVISING, MODIFYING AND CUSTOMIZING PLANS

Like many homeowners who buy these plans, you and your builder, architect or engineer may want to make changes to them. We recommend purchase of a reproducible plan for any changes made by your builder, licensed architect or engineer. As set forth below, we cannot assume any responsibility for blueprints which have been changed, whether by you, your builder or by professionals selected by you or referred to you by us, because such individuals are outside our supervision and control.

ARCHITECTURAL AND ENGINEERING SEALS

Some cities and states are now requiring that a licensed architect or engineer review and "seal" a blueprint, or officially approve it, prior to construction due to concerns over energy costs, safety and other factors. Prior to application for a building permit or the start of actual construction, we strongly advise that you consult your local building official who can tell you if such a review is required.

ABOUT THE DESIGNS

The architects and designers whose work appears in this publication are among America's leading residential designers. Each plan was designed to meet the requirements of a nationally recognized model building code in effect at the time and place the plan was drawn. Because national building codes change from time to time, plans may not comply with any such code at the time they are sold to a customer. In addition, building officials may not accept these plans as final construction documents of record as the plans may need to be modified and additional drawings and details added to suit local conditions and requirements. We strongly advise that purchasers consult a licensed architect or engineer, and their local building official, before starting any construction related to these plans.

LOCAL BUILDING CODES AND ZONING REQUIREMENTS

At the time of creation, our plans are drawn to specifications published by the Building Officials and Code Administrators (BOCA) International, Inc.; the Southern Building Code Congress (SBCCI) International, Inc.; the International Conference of Building Officials (ICBO); or the Council of American Building Officials (CABO). Our plans are designed to meet or exceed national building standards. Because of the great differences in geography and climate throughout the United States and Canada, each state, county and municipality has its own building codes, zone requirements, ordinances and building regulations. Your plan may need to be modified to comply with local requirements regarding snow loads, energy codes, soil and seismic conditions and a wide range of other matters. In addition, you may need to obtain permits or inspections from local governments before and in the course of construction. Prior to using blueprints ordered from us, we strongly advise that you consult a licensed architect or engineer—and speak with your local building official—before applying for any permit or beginning construction. We authorize the use of our blueprints on the express condition that you strictly comply with all local building codes, zoning requirements and other applicable laws, regulations, ordinances and requirements. Notice: Plans for homes to be built in Nevada must be re-drawn by a Nevada-registered professional. Consult your building official for more information on this subject.

TOLL FREE
1-800-521-6797

REGULAR OFFICE HOURS:

8:00 a.m.-9:00 p.m. EST, Monday-Friday

If we receive your order by 3:00 p.m. EST, Monday-Friday, we'll process it and ship within **two business days**. When ordering by phone, please have your credit card or check information ready. We'll also ask you for the Order Form Key Number at the bottom of the order form.

By FAX: Copy the Order Form on the next page and send it on our FAX line: 1-800-224-6699 or 520-544-3086.

Canadian Customers
Order Toll Free 1-877-223-6389

DISCLAIMER

The designers we work with have put substantial care and effort into the creation of their blueprints. However, because they cannot provide on-site consultation, supervision and control over actual construction, and because of the great variance in local building requirements, building practices and soil, seismic, weather and other conditions, WE CANNOT MAKE ANY WARRANTY, EXPRESS OR IMPLIED, WITH RESPECT TO THE CONTENT OR USE OF THE BLUEPRINTS, INCLUDING BUT NOT LIMITED TO ANY WARRANTY OF MERCHANTABILITY OR OF FITNESS FOR A PARTICULAR PURPOSE. **ITEMS, PRICES, TERMS AND CONDITIONS ARE SUBJECT TO CHANGE WITHOUT NOTICE. REPRODUCIBLE PLAN ORDERS MAY REQUIRE A CUSTOMER'S SIGNED RELEASE BEFORE SHIPPING.**

TERMS AND CONDITIONS

These designs are protected under the terms of United States Copyright Law and may not be copied or reproduced in any way, by any means, unless you have purchased Reproducibles which clearly indicate your right to copy or reproduce. We authorize the use of your chosen design as an aid in the construction of one single family home only. You may not use this design to build a second or multiple dwellings without purchasing another blueprint or blueprints or paying additional design fees.

HOW MANY BLUEPRINTS DO YOU NEED?

Although a standard building package may satisfy many states, cities and counties, some plans may require certain changes. For your convenience, we have developed a Reproducible plan which allows a local professional to modify and make up to 10 copies of your revised plan. As our plans are all copyright protected, with your purchase of the Reproducible, we will supply you with a Copyright release letter. The number of copies you may need: 1 for owner; 3 for builder; 2 for local building department and 1-3 sets for your mortgage lender.

📞 ORDER TOLL FREE!

**For information about
any of our services
or to order call
1-800-521-6797**

**Browse our website:
www.eplans.com**

**BLUEPRINTS ARE
NOT REFUNDABLE
EXCHANGES ONLY**

**For Customer Service,
call toll free
1-888-690-1116.**

HOME PLANNERS, LLC
Wholly owned by Hanley-Wood, LLC
3275 WEST INA ROAD, SUITE 110
® **TUCSON, ARIZONA 85741**

THE BASIC BLUEPRINT PACKAGE
Rush me the following (please refer to the Plans Index and Price Schedule in this section):

_____ Set(s) of reproducibles*, plan number(s) _____ $_____

_____ Set(s) of blueprints, plan number(s) _____ $_____

_____ Additional identical blueprints (standard or reverse) in same order @ $50 per set $_____

_____ Sets of Gazebo Construction Details @ $14.95 per set. $_____

_____ Sets of Complete Construction Package (Best Buy!) Add $10 to Building Package
Includes Custom Plan _____
Plus Deck or Gazebo Construction Details $_____

IMPORTANT EXTRA
Rush me the following:
_____ Specification Outlines @ $10 each $_____

POSTAGE AND HANDLING (signature is required for all deliveries)		
CARRIER DELIVERY	**1–3 sets**	**4+ sets**
No CODs (Requires street address—No P.O.Boxes)		
• **Regular Service** (Allow 7–10 business days for delivery)	❑ $20.00	❑ $25.00
• **Priority** (Allow 4–5 business days for delivery)	❑ $25.00	❑ $35.00
• **Express** (Allow 3 business days for delivery)	❑ $35.00	❑ $55.00
Overseas Delivery	Phone, FAX or Mail for Quote	

NOTE: All delivery times are from date blueprint package is shipped.

POSTAGE (from box above) $ _____

SUBTOTAL $ _____

SALES TAX (AZ & MI residents, please add appropriate state & local sales tax.) $ _____

TOTAL (Subtotal and Tax) $ _____

YOUR ADDRESS (please print legibly)

Name _____

Street _____

City _____ State _____ ZIP _____

Daytime telephone number (required) _____

* Fax number (required for reproducible orders) _____

TeleCheck® Checks By Phone℠ available

FOR CREDIT CARD ORDERS ONLY Please fill in the information below:

Credit card number _____ Exp: Month/Year_____

Check One: ❑ Visa ❑ MasterCard ❑ Discover Card ❑ American Express

Signature (required)_____

Please check appropriate box: ❑ Licensed Builder-Contractor ❑ Homeowner

📞 ORDER TOLL FREE
1-800-521-6797

BY FAX: Copy the order form above and send it on our
FAXLINE: 1-800-224-6699 or 520-544-3086

| Order Form Key |
| HPT282 |

1 BIGGEST & BEST

1001 of our best-selling plans in one volume. 1,074 to 7,275 square feet. 704 pgs $12.95 1K1

2 ONE-STORY

450 designs for all lifestyles. 800 to 4,900 square feet. 384 pgs $9.95 OS

3 MORE ONE-STORY

475 superb one-level plans from 800 to 5,000 square feet. 448 pgs $9.95 MO2

4 TWO-STORY

443 designs for one-and-a-half and two stories. 1,500 to 6,000 square feet. 448 pgs $9.95 TS

5 VACATION

430 designs for recreation, retirement and leisure. 448 pgs $9.95 VS3

6 HILLSIDE

208 designs for split-levels, bi-levels, multi-levels and walkouts. 224 pgs $9.95 HH

7 FARMHOUSE

300 Fresh Designs from Classic to Modern. 320 pgs. $10.95 FCP

8 COUNTRY HOUSES

208 unique home plans that combine traditional style and modern livability. 224 pgs $9.95 CN

9 BUDGET-SMART

200 efficient plans from 7 top designers, that you can really afford to build! 224 pgs $8.95 BS

10 BARRIER-FREE

Over 1,700 products and 51 plans for accessible living. 128 pgs $15.95 UH

11 ENCYCLOPEDIA

500 exceptional plans for all styles and budgets—the best book of its kind! 528 pgs $9.95 ENC

12 ENCYCLOPEDIA II

500 completely new plans. Spacious and stylish designs for every budget and taste. 352 pgs $9.95 E2

13 AFFORDABLE

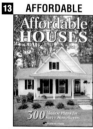

300 Modest plans for savvy homebuyers.256 pgs. $9.95 AH2

14 VICTORIAN

210 striking Victorian and Farmhouse designs from today's top designers. 224 pgs $15.95 VDH2

15 ESTATE

Dream big! Eighteen designers showcase their biggest and best plans. 224 pgs $16.95 EDH3

16 LUXURY

170 lavish designs, over 50% brand-new plans added to a most elegant collection. 192 pgs $12.95 LD3

17 EUROPEAN STYLES

200 homes with a unique flair of the Old World. 224 pgs $15.95 EURO

18 COUNTRY CLASSICS

Donald Gardner's 101 best Country and Traditional home plans. 192 pgs $17.95 DAG

19 COUNTRY

85 Charming Designs from American Home Gallery. 160 pgs. $17.95 CTY

20 TRADITIONAL

85 timeless designs from the Design Traditions Library. 160 pgs $17.95 TRA

21 COTTAGES

245 Delightful retreats from 825 to 3,500 square feet. 256 pgs. $10.95 COOL

22 CABINS TO VILLAS

Enchanting Homes for Mountain Sea or Sun, from the Sater collection. 144 pgs $19.95 CCV

23 CONTEMPORARY

The most complete and imaginative collection of contemporary designs available anywhere. 256 pgs $10.95 CM2

24 FRENCH COUNTRY

Live every day in the French countryside using these plans, landscapes and interiors. 192 pgs $14.95 PN

25 SOUTHERN

207 homes rich in Southern styling and comfort. 240 pgs $8.95 SH

26 SOUTHWESTERN

138 designs that capture the spirit of the Southwest. 144 pgs $10.95 SW

27 SHINGLE-STYLE

155 Home plans from Classic Colonials to Breezy Bungalows. 192 pgs. $12.95 SNG

28 NEIGHBORHOOD

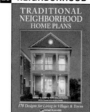

170 designs with the feel of main street America. 192 pgs $12.95 TND

29 CRAFTSMAN

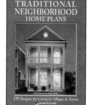

170 Home plans in the Craftsman and Bungalow style. 192 pgs $12.95 CC

30 GRAND VISTAS

200 Homes with a View. 224 pgs. $10.95 GV

Home Planners wants your building experience to be as pleasant and trouble-free as possible.
That's why we've expanded our library of do-it-yourself titles to help you along.

31 DUPLEX & TOWNHOMES
115 Duplex, Multiplex & Townhome Designs. 128 pgs. $17.95 MFH

32 WATERFRONT
200 designs perfect for your waterside wonderland. 208 pgs $10.95 WF

33 NATURAL LIGHT
223 Sunny home plans for all regions. 240 pgs. $8.95 NA

34 NOSTALGIA
100 Time-Honored designs updated with today's features. 224 pgs. $14.95 NOS

35 STREET OF DREAMS
Over 300 photos showcase 54 prestigious homes. 256 pgs $19.95 SOD

36 NARROW-LOT
250 Designs for houses 17' to 50' wide. 256 pgs. $9.95 NL2

37 SMALL HOUSES
Innovative plans for sensible lifestyles. 224 pgs. $8.95 SM2

38 GARDENS & MORE
225 gardens, landscapes, decks and more to enhance every home. 320 pgs. $19.95 GLP

39 EASY-CARE
41 special landscapes designed for beauty and low maintenance. 160 pgs $14.95 ECL

40 BACKYARDS
40 designs focused solely on creating your own specially themed backyard oasis. 160 pgs $14.95 BYL

41 BEDS & BORDERS
40 Professional designs for do-it-yourselfers. 160 pgs. $14.95 BB

42 BUYER'S GUIDE
A comprehensive look at 2700 products for all aspects of landscaping & gardening. 128 pgs $19.95 LPBG

LANDSCAPE DESIGNS

43 OUTDOOR
74 easy-to-build designs, lets you create and build your own backyard oasis. 128 pgs $9.95 YG2

44 GARAGES
145 exciting projects from 64 to 1,900 square feet. 160 pgs. $9.95 GG2

45 DECKS
A brand new collection of 120 beautiful and practical decks. 144 pgs. $9.95 DP2

46 HOME BUILDING
Everything you need to know to work with contractors and subcontractors. 212 pgs $14.95 HBP

47 RURAL BUILDING
Everything you need to know to build your home in the country. 232 pgs. $14.95 BYC

48 VACATION HOMES
Your complete guide to building your vacation home. 224 pgs. $14.95 BYV

PROJECT GUIDES

Book Order Form

To order your books, just check the box of the book numbered below and complete the coupon. We will process your order and ship it from our office within two business days. Send coupon and check (in U.S. funds).

YES! Please send me the books I've indicated:

❑ 1:1K1 ....$12.95	❑ 17:EURO...$15.95	❑ 33:NA..........$8.95
❑ 2:OS............$9.95	❑ 18:DAG $17.95	❑ 34:NOS $14.95
❑ 3:MO2..........$9.95	❑ 19:CTY......$17.95	❑ 35:SOD $19.95
❑ 4:TS $9.95	❑ 20:TRA......$17.95	❑ 36:NL2........$9.95
❑ 5:VS3..........$9.95	❑ 21:COOL....$10.95	❑ 37:SM2........$8.95
❑ 6:HH...........$9.95	❑ 22:CCV......$19.95	❑ 38:GLP......$19.95
❑ 7:FCP.......$10.95	❑ 23:CM2......$10.95	❑ 39:ECL......$14.95
❑ 8:CN...........$9.95	❑ 24:PN........$14.95	❑ 40:BYL......$14.95
❑ 9:BS $8.95	❑ 25:SH.........$8.95	❑ 41:BB........$14.95
❑ 10:UH $15.95	❑ 26:SW........$10.95	❑ 42:LPBG....$19.95
❑ 11:ENC........$9.95	❑ 27:SNG.......$12.95	❑ 43:YG2........$9.95
❑ 12:E2..........$9.95	❑ 28:TND......$12.95	❑ 44:GG2........$9.95
❑ 13:AH2........$9.95	❑ 29:CC........$12.95	❑ 45:DP2........$9.95
❑ 14:VDH2...$15.95	❑ 30:GV........$10.95	❑ 46:HBP.....$14.95
❑ 15:EDH3 ...$16.95	❑ 31:MFH.....$17.95	❑ 47:BYC.....$14.95
❑ 16:LD3......$12.95	❑ 32:WF.......$10.95	❑ 48:BYV.....$14.95

Books Subtotal $_____
ADD Postage and Handling (allow 4–6 weeks for delivery) $ 4.00
Sales Tax: (AZ & MI residents, add state and local sales tax.) $_____
YOUR TOTAL (Subtotal, Postage/Handling, Tax) $_____

YOUR ADDRESS (PLEASE PRINT)

Name _____

Street _____

City _____ State _____ Zip _____

Phone (_____) _____ — _____

YOUR PAYMENT

TeleCheck® Checks By Phone℠ available

Check one: ❑ Check ❑ Visa ❑ MasterCard ❑ Discover ❑ American Express

Required credit card information:

Credit Card Number _____

Expiration Date (Month/Year)_____

Signature Required _____

Home Planners, LLC
3275 W. Ina Road, Suite 110, Dept. BK, Tucson, AZ 85741

HPT282

Canadian Customers Order Toll Free 1-877-223-6389

159

HOME PLANNING RESOURCES

For faster service order online at
www.hwspecials.com

Heat-N-Glo
1-888-427-3973
www.heatnglo.com

HEAT-N-GLO®
No one builds a better fire

Heat-N-Glo offers quality gas, woodburning and electric fireplaces, including gas log sets, stoves, and inserts for preexisting fireplaces. Now available gas grills and outdoor fireplaces. Send for a free brochure.

Style Solutions Incorporated

Ideas for your next project. Beautiful, durable, elegant low-maintenance millwork, mouldings, balustrade systems and much more. For your free catalog please call us at 1-800-446-3040 or visit www.stylesolutionsinc.com.

Aristokraft
One MasterBrand Cabinets Drive
Jasper, IN 47546
(812) 482-2527
www.aristokraft.com

Aristokraft® Cabinetry
Great Ideas Made Easy

Aristokraft offers you superb value, outstanding quality and great style that fit your budget. Transform your great ideas into reality with popular styles and features that reflect your taste and lifestyle. $5.00

Therma-Tru Doors
1687 Woodlands Drive
Maumee, OH 43537
1-800-THERMA-TRU
www.thermatru.com

THERMA TRU® DOORS
THE DOOR SYSTEM YOU CAN BELIEVE IN

The undisputed brand leader, Therma-Tru specializes in fiberglass and steel entry doors for every budget. Excellent craftsmanship, energy efficiency and variety make Therma-Tru the perfect choice for all your entry door needs.

225 Garden, Landscape and Project Plans
To order, call
1-800-322-6797

225 Do-It-Yourself designs that help transform boring yards into exciting outdoor entertainment spaces. Gorgeous gardens, luxurious landscapes, dazzling decks and other outdoor amenities. Complete construction blueprints available for every project. Only $19.95 (plus $4 shipping/handling).

Have we got plans for you!

eplans.com
Stop dreaming. Start building.

Your online source for home designs and ideas. Find thousands of plans from the nation's top designers...all in one place. Plus, links to the best known names in building supplies and services.

160